to
w
frightening journeys!
Michael Self
& Bonnie

A Journey of Work-Life Renewal

*The Power to Recharge & Rekindle
Passion in Your Life*

Bonnie Michaels / Michael Seef

Managing Work & Family, Inc.

Copyright © 2003 by Managing Work & Family, Inc.

All rights reserved.

Printed in the United States of America.

No part of this book may be used, reproduced, or transmitted in any form or by any means, electronic or mechanical, including photocopying, recording, or by any information storage or retrieval system—except by a reviewer who may quote brief passages in a review to be printed in a magazine or newspaper—without express written permission from the publisher. For information contact: Managing Work & Family Inc., 912 Crain Street, Evanston, IL, 60202

www.mwfam.com

While the authors and publisher have done everything possible to include a wide range of travel resources and information, we assume no liability or responsibility for inaccuracies, errors, omissions, and inconsistencies rendered in the creation of this book. Any slights of people or organizations are fully unintentional. When deciding upon travel, readers must use their own best judgment and consultation with others, if necessary, to maintain safety.

Publisher's Cataloging-in-Publication

(Provided by Quality Books, Inc.)

Michaels, Bonnie.
   A journey of work/life renewal : the power to recharge & rekindle passion in your life / by Bonnie Michaels and Michael Seef.
   p. cm.
   Includes bibliographical references.
   ISBN 0-9728115-0-8

1. Self-actualization (Psychology) 2. Quality of life. 3. Quality of work life. 4. Travel--Psychological aspects. 5. Flamenco. I. Seef, Michael. II. Title.

BF637.S4M53 2003   158

QBI33-1133

Printed in the United States of America

In Praise of *A Journey of Work-Life Renewal:*

Reading "A Journey of Work-Life Renewal" is an adventure in itself. Following the travels of Bonnie and Mike is inspirational, educational, and thought provoking—not to mention the useful hints. This book should give everyone who reads it the courage and knowledge necessary to enhance their lives and test their dreams. A fascinating read!—Cliff Lynch, C.F. Lynch & Assoc.

As you share Bonnie and Michael's outward global journey and their inner spiritual journey, you will gain amazing insights on how to create your own renewal plan. You'll discover a more joyful way to live. Don't leave home without this book! —Sharon Lloyd Spence, author, *Adventure Guide to Southeast Florida* and Senior Editor, www.greatestescapes.com

For those of us not able to take a long renewal trip, we can live vicariously through Bonnie and Michael's engaging tales of their wonderful journey. I now long to visit Seville for an extended time and have added it to my own "things to see along the way" list. This practical guide also points out ways to engage in spiritual renewal on a daily basis. "A Journey of Work-Life Renewal" inspires dreaming again–on many levels. Thank you, Bonnie and Michael!—C. Elizabeth McCarty, co-author, "Solving the Work-Family Puzzle."

"A Journey of Work-Life Renewal" represents an authentic and honest experience of sabbatical with different options for renewing our passion. It will be one of the books in my library with tattered edges that I refer to again and again in my personal and professional life.—Cynthia Kulik, Organization Development Consultant.

Bonnie Michaels' "A Journey of Work-Life Renewal" is like a great meal– one wonderful course after another, as these two generous adventurers allow us to come along as they experience their renewal. Beautifully writtten, this fascinating read is also a step-by-step guide to our own renewal, giving us the courage, the inspiration, and the knowledge to experiment with our own lives.—Susan Seitel, Work-Family Connections

This is the rare book that makes you think about the possibilities that life may hold for you, challenges you to think about what you can do, and then to DO IT!—Christine Rossman, Corporate Work/Life Manager

Filled with insightful and intriguing adventures sure to strike a chord in armchair travelers and road warriors alike! Part travelogue, part how-to, this book weaves tales of the couple's year-long sabbatical in Spain, Israel, Japan, Thailand, and Australia. Even if you've never considered taking time-off from your life and work–odds are you will after reading "A Journey of Work-Life Renewal."—Candice Hadley, President, Hadley Enterprises.

A Journey of Work-Life Renewal
The Power to Recharge & Rekindle Passion in Your Life

Bonnie Michaels / Michael Seef

Managing Work & Family, Inc.

Published by:
Managing Work & Family, Inc.
912 Crain Street
Evanston, IL, 60202

Order Information
To order more copies contact: Bonnie Michaels
E-mail: mwfam@aol.com
Phone: 847-864-0916
www.mwfam.com

Bonnie Michaels is an internationally recognized work-life consultant, speaker, author and President of *Managing Work & Family, Inc.* A sought after keynote speaker and workshop leader, she motivates individuals to make change and live a balanced life. Ms. Michaels has worked with corporations and associations for over fifteen years to effectively identify and solve their work-life issues.

Ms. Michaels has appeared on CNN and other network news magazine programs and frequently authors articles on work-life issues for magazines, newspapers and trade publications.

Ms. Michaels is passionate about her life and preserves a sense of adventure. Bonnie Michaels has also authored, *Solving the Work/Family Puzzle,* Business One Irwin, 1992.

Michael Seef is an expert in logistics and product distribution. As president of *MDS Logistics*, he works with Fortune 500 and smaller companies both domestically and internationally. Michael's experience in international work is extensive, and he is fluent in German and conversational in Spanish. He has degrees in economics and engineering. Michael's passion for the outdoors includes bicycling, hiking, and nature.

As a result of their unique year-off, they now offer workshops and speeches on the preparation and execution of "time-off." They have been married for fifteen years and have three children and five grandchildren.

This book is dedicated to all those who have ventured on the path less traveled.

Acknowledgments:

A journey is often inspired by others who have gone before. We are most grateful to Marina and T.L Eovaldi and Susan and Michael Antman who spent many hours sharing their experiences and giving us courage.

The journey could not have easily taken place without those at home taking care of our affairs. We are grateful to Kaylyn and Len LoCoco, Judy Chiss, Bernie Cohen, Mark and Sheryl Seef and Phil and Terry Lanier. Tammy Maddrey made it possible to keep the work flowing and Michael Scott and Mary Ellen Gornick filled in during my absence.

Our story has been greatly enhanced by our editor, Donald Altman, who was able to see our vision.

Finally, there would be no stories if not for all the meaningful encounters with total strangers who gave of their friendship, time and trust. In a world of great chaos and mistrust, it is reaffirming to know that you can travel across the world safely.

Table of Contents

1. First Destination: Living Your Passion ... 1
2. Creating a New Life from Scratch ... 11
3. Changing Cultures, Changing Emotions ... 31
4. Going Solo ... 44
5. Staying Connected ... 59
6. Changing Course ... 69
7. Taking a Vacation from Your Time-Off ... 78
8. Being Useful and Volunteering Down Under ... 86
9. Work Camps, Rice Balls, and Bowing ... 104
10. Re-entry Blues and Renewal ... 125
11. Making Your Decision ... 149
12. Successfully Pulling the Plug ... 175
13. Renewal Tips, Workshops, and Resources ... 203

Chapter 1

First Destination: Living Your Passion

Dare to dream that you are more than the sum of your current circumstances.

—The Monk Who Sold His Ferrari

*T*he church bells toll at nine. It is my wake up call. Slowly, I emerge from the bedcovers and remember I don't have to do anything but to enjoy the day—relish in the sights and delights of Seville. At first there are feelings of guilt, but these soon dissolve in the sheer joy I feel at having unlimited free time. I'm intoxicated by the smells of orange blossoms, fresh bread, garlic, and coffee. The sounds of church bells and a continuous stream of lively animated conversation surround me. I feel the warm Spanish sun on my back. I see piercing blue skies above me. I'm perfectly content to be in the moment—taking in everything around me. I see, hear, watch, and listen. I speak infrequently. As I sit for hours in a park or cafe, I realize how badly I have needed to do "nothing." Every now and then I pinch myself. My dream of living in Seville for months at a time is really here.

Then I remember my reason for taking time-off from work and family responsibilities. Doing nothing in these circumstances means no structured life, but being active in other ways. In truth, I am growing stronger inside, healing my spirit, learning more. *A Journey of Work-Life Renewal* is about who I am, and even living my dream of studying flamenco dancing.

Here in Seville, life is different. People do work and raise families, but they also take time for siestas, time for friends, and time for strolling with no particular goal in mind. There is time for pleasantries and casual conversation. It is very renewing after years of scheduling every minute of my time with activities. Still, there are moments when I consider my greatest fear: That I will never again want to go back to my family and work responsibilities. I also wonder how I will take this knowledge and experience back home with me when my yearlong journey is over. But I'm getting ahead of myself.

Unvarnished Truth About Time-Off

Let me share with you the unvarnished truth about the myth of taking time-off: Time-off to renew isn't for the extraordinary person. It's for anyone who needs to rejuvenate the spirit, mind, and body! Step outside of yourself for awhile—be a kid and imagine your dreams ready to be filled.

It really is possible. Do you have a dream to fulfill? Do you ever wish you could embark on your dream *now*, before you retire? Do you ever imagine what life without work will be like?

A Journey of Work-Life Renewal takes you through the joys, disappointments, and surprises of leaving a safe, structured work-life for a year into the unknown for renewal. Renewal means taking control over your time—to let go, step out of the comfort zone, and to recharge and rekindle your passion for life. With a clear purpose and plan, a journey of work-life renewal can enrich your life and even your relationships. That was certainly the case for myself and my traveling companion (and husband) Michael.

Our unique encounters with life around the world may prompt you to reflect on your life and provide you with creative solutions to get renewed. You'll be treated to many heartwarming and sometimes amusing stories as we stumble and make our way around the world with little more than one suitcase each—and a modest budget to match.

Now that I have disconnected with my old life, I can hardly believe the words I once spoke in denial: "Time-off for renewal? I don't need it. I'm perfectly fine. I'm a work-life balance expert and I know how to keep in balance." Yet, the years of raising children, caring for grandchildren and elders, and starting a business all take its toll—not to mention giving so much to others in my consulting practice. When you are burned out and lose passion, you lose the core of you. Our lifestyles in the US offer very little for renewal opportunities—long working hours and stress are the norm.

We invite you along on our journey around the globe as we explore the passions in our hearts and the struggles that challenge us to grow. We hope this journey will inspire you, as well as give you all the practical tools you'll need to take the road less traveled. Time is a gift, and dreams wait for no one. Time is now. Make that *your* time is now!

Unplugging for Your Journey

It takes courage to seek meaningful time-off. Michael and I had many fears before taking the road less traveled. For example, Michael wasn't feeling the same emotional stress as I, and he needed to be convinced. Along with our adventures, *A Journey of Work-Life Renewal* outlines the concerns, issues, and planning you'll need to consider each step of the way. We elaborate in detail all the many tasks involved leading up to the yearlong trip we took around the world.

Pursuing passions and experiencing the simple joys of life and letting go are covered in chapter 2, *Creating a New Life From Scratch*. Here, we learn how to use our resources to develop a satisfying network of Spanish and international friends. In addition, you'll learn how to use mindfulness and awareness as a tool to help you adjust to different cultural norms. This chapter also illustrates how roles between traveling companions can go topsy-turvy. You'll get an example of how adapting is necessary for renewal growth, especially when Michael takes on the unexpected role of what I fondly call a PSP, or Passion Support Person.

No journey description would be completely honest without sharing the ups and downs. In chapter 3, *Changing Cultures, Changing Emotions*, a challenging archaeological dig in Israel offers an example of how emotions are heightened as we dig into the past of our ancestors as well as our own. My husband was born in Israel, and my daughter was born in Jerusalem after the six-day war. This exotic and biblical setting provides a framework for exploring the ups and downs which a couple faces when traveling together for a whole year. There is even a section that describes how we solved the problem of opposing objectives by living a month apart—each doing what we needed to do to fulfill strong emotional needs in different countries. You will learn about the positive results of that decision, and how the process helped us grow as a couple, as well as individually.

Going Solo, chapter 4, explores what it's like to take meaningful time-off by yourself. In addition to many helpful hints for solo travel, this chapter illustrates that time alone can also be time for you to gain new confidence, stretch your wings, and soar to new heights.

Just because your renewal time takes you to the other side of the world doesn't mean you can't communicate with family and friends back home, not to mention those you've met along the way. In chapter 5, *Staying Connected*, you'll learn the secrets of how-to stay in touch, whether you are computer literate or not. Some of the greatest joys of our journey were the many individuals who influenced us along the way and have now become a regular part of our lives via e-mail.

Chapter 6, *Changing Course*, takes you along on what turns out to be a spiritual journey. A spiritual quest sometimes brings to the surface emotions and feelings that can't always be anticipated. Our experience and practical tips will help you discover some useful ways for making a spiritual journey an integral part of your meaningful time-off.

Chapter 7, *Taking a Vacation from Your Time-Off*, illuminates another facet of taking meaningful time-off. Sometimes you have to just kick back and relax, with no agenda or objective in sight!

In chapter 8, *Being Useful and Volunteering Down Under*, you'll discover what it's like to volunteer for room and board in a foreign land. We did this for the Willing Workers of Organic Farms in Australia and the Volunteers for Peace in Japan. One story involves experiences of living and working in an Aborigine and mining community in the middle of a desert in Western Australia.

Chapter 9, *Work Camps, Rice Balls, and Bowing*, focuses on the humor of being middle-aged and living and working with young people (ages 19-25) in a bungalow in a forest of southwestern Japan. Believe me when I say it wasn't easy. But there are many heart-warming stories of how new friendships and volunteering work can lead to personal growth and development. In addition, this chapter shares other sources for finding volunteer opportunities around the world.

What happened when we got back to the US? I can only be honest in stating that reentry was tough. Chapter 10, *Re-Entry Blues and Renewal*, portrays the re-entry process and provides suggestions to make it easier for others. We clarify the personal changes that have occurred since our renewal time and how we integrate them into our personal and professional lives since coming back. There's also an *Addendum* that brings to life the creativity that followed the reentry period by providing you with a list of workshops that were developed as the result of the time-off experience. Finally, you will find a long list of resources to help as you restart and renew your own life.

To encourage adventure travel, our journey includes vivid descriptions of special trips—to Spain, Israel, Sinai, Australia, Germany, Switzerland, and Japan—that teach, inspire, challenge, and promote spiritual and intellectual growth. These trips brought unexpected dividends that continue to enrich our life and work today.

The closing two chapters give you an opportunity to examine your own barriers to taking time for renewal. These chapters, *Making Your Decision* and *Successfully Pulling the Plug*, include everything from helping you develop goals and strategies to expertly guiding you with an extensive twelve-month Time Line Chart. This chart lays the groundwork for your trip with a practical and comprehensive step-by-step plan that covers all these essentials: Finances, house preparation and rental, packing, setting up communications, checking on health and insurance programs, setting up means for business continuation, and researching country, language, and volunteer opportunities.

How Renewal Helped Us with September 11, 2001

When the events of September 11, 2001 unfolded, I found myself more resilient than most of my friends and colleagues. I realized that not only had I been renewed but I was more confident in dealing with the unknown. During the year's journey, I had faced myself, confronted my fears, and handled many difficult situations. As a result I am definitely stronger and ready to problem solve at a moments notice. If something should happen, I am more able to get by with fewer creature comforts and survive quite well. I realize that this crisis was quite different but the skills and attitudes used to deal with the issues are the same.

As the result of my renewal experience, I was also able to help others by taking action. For example, I mobilized my thoughts immediately and wrote a *Toolkit for Employers on Handling the National Crisis*, produced by Family Support America.

As to the future, if 9-11 teaches us anything it is not to stop living. At the same time, you need to be prepared when you travel and make good decisions about where and when. Personally, I have not stopped enjoying life and traveling. However, I pay attention and am alert. We had a lot practice on our trip. The best preparation is in the mind. It is believing in yourself and your ability to handle anything that comes your way. It is being steady in thought and action.

Threats from abroad continue to instill fear. We all make choices about dealing with them. One can obsess on them or take a different tact—acknowledge them and then know you have some control. Live each moment of the day fully. Accept what you can't change. Fulfill your dreams now.

I believe that there is no substitute for extended time away from routines and comfortable, familiar settings. However, upon returning, I realize some individuals won't or can't pull the plug on their lives, so in the Resources section I offer suggestions on ways to get renewed without going away that are based on what I learned from my journey. It provides readers with ideas for changing their lives and a model for making it happen.

How has meaningful time-off made a difference in my life? I now know so much more about my intuitive feelings for needing extended time-off. It has changed life for both my husband and I. The rewards are far greater than just renewed energy for work and personal life. Personally, I have benefited from learning about myself and about others in different cultures. I feel that I can handle any new difficulty that will show up in my life. I am shining inside and outside with a new glow and joy for life again. I am stronger emotionally and physically. I am more appreciative of the little things around me. Fortunately, you too can use the power of life renewal to balance and re-energize your life with new purpose and meaning.

More than ever before, people need renewal time. "A successful life has become a violent enterprise—war on our bodies, family and community," says Wayne Muller, author of *Sabbath*. "As the workforce continues to work longer hours, individuals are often stressed. The busier we are, the more important we seem to ourselves, and we imagine, to others." This well-described pattern of behavior results in burn out, lack of passion about work, and not living honestly within one's true values. If you are one of the chronically anxious, you are not alone. Here are some questions that may help you evaluate your own personal Renewal and Passion Quotient.

Passion and Renewal Quotient Questionnaire

Are you ready for time-off? Answer the following questions honestly and objectively. Score 1 point for each statement you answer with a "yes."

After answering the questionnaire, take time to consider your feelings about the questions that follow each statement. You may even want to write down your feelings and reflections in your own Renewal Journal.

1. I am often bored with my current job.
   What is my true passion, and how can it be revived by renewal time-off?

2. I am feeling unenthusiastic about my current lifestyle.
   How would you describe your lifestyle? What would you change?

3. I often work more than 8 hours a day.
   When was the last time you had one whole day of unstructured time?

4. I would like to simplify my life and rid my self of the burnout or high levels of stress.
   When was the last time you lived without an alarm, TV or phone, or the last time you traveled with very few possessions?

5. I often daydream about taking time-off for myself.
   What is your definition of success? Who/what is your authentic self?

6. I often lose patience with friends, family, and co-workers.
   Do you whine if you are put in some physical discomfort—too hot, too cold, have to wait?

7. My company has gone through changes in the last several years such as downsizing, a merger, or buyout.
   Do you feel apathetic about some aspects of your life?

8. I often question the meaning of my life, or would like to devote more time to developing my spiritual life.
   What would be a satisfying spiritual quest for you?

9. I am retired and feel the passion for life is not the same as when I was working.

10. I would like to apply myself to learning a new skill, craft or subject.
    What new skill or craft would you love to learn?

11. I would love to have some chunks of uninterrupted and unstructured time.

12. I would like to live my life more authentically in tune with my values.
    What values do you admire the most?

13. I feel my attitude toward money is driving my life.
    If you have children, how can time-off revitalize family life?

If you answered yes to five or more of these statements, then you are ready to hit the pause button and renew your life in a new direction.

Chapter 2

Creating a New Life From Scratch

Life loves to be taken by the lapel and told "I'm with you kid, Let's go!"

—Maya Angelou

You can't be laid back all the time and wait for life to come to you on a renewal journey. We have settled into our tiny Seville apartment in Spain, the first of many countries we will visit on our renewal journey. Now what? Exploring and doing nothing is great but we soon realize that we need a daily routine. However, one that better fits the Spanish lifestyle, which is lived outdoors. Food and drink are very important here and socializing at outdoor cafes is a daily occurrence—unlike the US way of life. So with whom will you be social? And while we enjoy each other's company, there is a need for a broader social life. After only a week in our apartment, a typical routine takes shape. Breakfast is followed by a leisurely stroll, coffee in a cafe, food shopping, lunch, siesta (stores close from 2 P.M.-5 P.M.), coffee in another cafe, exploring, tapas, dinner, and music. We go to bed when we are tired. There is no clock to set. We have no TV, so reading is a vital part of our life.

To get us moving along with our renewal process, we need to find some classes. Our small network of Jorge and Lucy (a tailor's son and Australian girlfriend) not only help us, but act as important role models in our quest for authenticity. They each possess enormous courage in their relationship despite cultural differences. With their help we arrange for a Spanish tutor twice a week. Our tutor, by the way, is from Argentina and displays incredible resourcefulness, adaptability, and spirit. Next, we begin the long-awaited but arduous task of finding a flamenco teacher.

Thanks to Michael's many phone calls in broken Spanish and excursions around the city to many out-of-the way studios, we finally locate one. Now our daily life has more of a focus and includes classes, Spanish homework, and flamenco foot practice. We enjoy our language study in sunny surroundings in the parks, by the Guadalquivir River, and outdoor cafes—the Spanish way.

My flamenco classes began to provide an international, English-speaking network. We share stories about our families, professions and why we are in Seville. Later on, by chance, I discover the American Women's Association, which provides a wealth of information, networks, activities, and good English-speaking company. Meanwhile, my adventurous husband answers an ad for a "fifty percent English-fifty percent Spanish" conversation partner and meets Margarita, a lovely, intelligent, journalism student. Margarita's dedication to learning is shown by extending herself for us. We are amazed at her courage to develop a deep relationship with us. Her trust, curiosity, and warmth are like that of a daughter. Even now, she continues to brighten our life with her correspondence. With her generosity and limited time, she introduces us to some of her male friends and our network of contacts expands. Eventually, we are invited to her home to meet her parents and sister—a real Spanish honor. Our social life is expanding.

To enjoy daily life and learn Spanish culture, we have to be inventive, adventuresome and assertive. We seize every opportunity for meeting people. For example, Carla shows us how it is possible to find a new passion later in one's life. As a former, famous flamenco dancer, she now transfers her creativity and energy into painting. Her love of dance recreated through her painting of flamenco dancers.

The city awaits us. We steep ourselves in learning more about the history and culture of Southern Spain (Andalusia). Our weekly routines include sight seeing, day trips and weekend sojourns. We soon discover where lists of events are printed in local papers. We soak in the exotic ambiance of local museums, churches, special exhibitions, music and dance at a leisurely pace. This is a true luxury of a life renewal. To explore our surroundings, we take delight in walking everywhere and, when needed, we take advantage of an excellent local bus system. We soon learn the ropes for finding the ins and outs of city busses and trains.

We are feeling stimulated and productive under the routines we have set. We even do more than we expected, and in such a short time, we have connected with others. Part of the journey is to drink in and absorb the unique ways in which our new acquaintances choose to live. When you have more time, you can begin to appreciate and deepen your understanding of others. For example, the tailor and his son exhibit great love for their profession. Watching the bond of respect between father and son was touching. Their mutual devotion to an important craft carries on a family tradition and honored skill, which is highly valued in Spain. What a contrast to our orientation in the US, where things new and high-tech are revered! It was meaningful to experience these shared values.

When you have your renewal experience, how will you establish a new life in your destination? You may discover that you need a routine or you may prefer a totally unstructured life or something in between. Where and how will you meet people? Each country is unique in this regard as you will discover in other chapters. Seville is an open and friendly city.

Consider joining a group that offers activities that you are interested in. For example, I joined a hiking group and met many locals who were happy to put up with my stilted Spanish. This active, social lifestyle may contribute to the fact that Spain has the lowest suicide rates in Europe, with a high life expectancy of 74.4 years for males and 81.6 years for females. Whatever you decide, try to connect with something you love. Surely, you will find others who share your passion—whether it is an obsession for fine wines, historical sites, or in my case, dancing.

Flamenco, Carmelita, and the Authentic Life

"Gotta dance, gotta dance." Gene Kelly said it and I cannot help but follow his lead. Okay, I admit that I am a flamenco addict. Ever since I discovered this haunting and mesmerizing music, I felt challenged to dance it. I haven't been the same since I donned the hard, nailed shoes and flamboyant skirts. Why flamenco? Everyone asks me this. It is one of the most difficult dance styles to understand and perform. Flamenco is a type of song, music, and dance that has origins with the Andalusian gypsies and was also influenced by Eastern Indian and Jewish cultures. It is all about the heart—deep feelings of love despair, anger, and joy. It is generally regarded as gypsy music—gypsy lament. It springs from a well of sorrow, yet raises one to great heights of ecstatic joy.

For me, flamenco poses a great, if not daunting, challenge. It requires enormous understanding of rhythmic patterns that have no melodic lines. It takes all my concentration to hear the *compas* (counts in the music) or contra time (the beats that go against the compas).

Physically, it requires my feet to pound out the rhythm while counting. For a middle-aged woman, this is a challenge. Most importantly, it demands that I dig deeply into my emotions. Anyone, in order to dance well, must be prepared to express emotions honestly while performing complex feats with hands, arms, and feet. Is this my authentic self? I only know that because of a lifelong dream, I have left behind the security of life in the quiet midwestern university town of Evanston, Illinois.

"*Hola. Mi marida neccessita una profesora de flamenco. Puede ayuda me, por favor?*"

Translation: "Hello. My wife needs a flamenco teacher. Can you help me, please?"

After Michael called and we visited a dozen flamenco studios (I had little Spanish vocabulary), I found Carmelita. Even on the phone, I could imagine her exuberance. She spoke in ways my American ears are not used to—with unbounded energy, emotion, passion, and laughter. And, gratefully, she spoke English.

It seemed a long way to her studio the first time—through twisting, narrow, and tiny cobblestone streets. The heavy wooden door of the studio was splintered with age. There was no bell—only *Infantes 9* written in small print. With trepidation, I knocked once and then knocked again. My heart pounded while I stood waiting. Needless to say, I was quite nervous. As a fifty-seven-year-old flamenco novice, I wondered how would I communicate and fit in? Then Carmelita appeared with her beautiful mane of chestnut hair, black laughing eyes, sparkling teeth, a stunning body, and a warm welcome. Feeling very shy and uncomfortable, I slowly walked in. My husband, who had accompanied me, soon said *adios*. Now I was alone and feeling very insecure. Before long, Fifi, Carmelita's white miniature poodle greeted me and broke the ice. She is the mascot of the studio and visits us frequently during dancing.

Carmelita waved me into the studio with a rush of words (Spanish and English), gestures, and a swoop of her dancing skirt. The rectangular studio was small, with walls of peeling paint and posters, but full of life—voices, foot practice, shouting, and music. I quickly jumped into the throng of energy and others greeted me with HOLA!

That was the beginning of my love affair with Carmelita's class. As the weeks passed, I discovered I could keep up with many of the younger, experienced students in spite of my middle-aged body. (Fortunately, introductory classes in the US helped to bridge some of the potential gaps.) With daily hard work, perseverance, and great intent, I began to master the complicated art form. The sense of accomplishment was overwhelming and contributed greatly to my renewal and self-confidence.

At times, it was hard to believe that I was living each day with pure joy and bliss. In retrospect, it was simple to do.

Children seem to master this. However, as adults, we often give in to cultural pressures and expectations that give us little pleasure. Will I be able to remember this lesson when I return home?

I soon found out I was not alone in my strange, almost obsessive pursuit of flamenco. I made some new acquaintances who were pursuing their passions and experimenting with other lifestyles as well. The international interest in flamenco is surprising. Most memorable was Gretta, a forty-year-old German woman, who gave up her job to risk dancing and organizing flamenco concerts in Hamburg. As a result of her perseverance, she brought Carmelita to Germany many times to teach and perform. Also impressive was a forty-year-old Swiss teacher on sabbatical. She was also responsible for keeping the flamenco connection alive. Upon returning to her home, she arranged for Carmelita to teach. A lively fifty-year-old Dutch performer refused to give in and danced despite many blisters and aches. She was always smiling as she tried to perfect her movements while in pain. In addition to these women, many young American and Japanese exchange students were also studying flamenco.

You may notice that many of the women are in their midlives—a time when individuals often begin the pursuit for authenticity and self-exploration. However, young or old, we all had something in common. We were all living our passion. It touched me to know that others shared my strong feelings. Trust yourself and know that someone will share your passion, too!

I learned a lot from Carmelita. In particular, I admire her intense and deep emotional involvement when dancing flamenco. She is a true role model. It isn't only her footwork, but her inner spirit and feelings that are so truthful when performing. Carmelita is genuine in all that she does. She lives her daily life with authenticity and emotional involvement—another lesson for me. She lives day-to-day, always true to herself and doesn't give in to outside pressures or "the shoulds." She somehow manages to earn a living by teaching and performing. She doesn't worry about tomorrow. Carmelita lives in the moment—fully and honestly.

She gives a lot to her friends and students by making time to be helpful. I spent many hours with Carmelita, both in and out of her studio. She included me in her family gatherings. We even had the pleasure of seeing a new love relationship unfold—one that was tested by distance and cultural obstacles. Watching her and her boyfriend jump over hurdles to be together deepened our appreciation for true love and commitment. When the pressures of life in the USA begin to affect me, I think about Carmelita and the authentic way of living.

Our relationship with Carmelita didn't dissipate, even after returning. We continue to correspond regularly and share the meaningful part of our lives. We even had a chance to meet her in Canada when she visited family living there. New friendships are one of the most rewarding aspects of our journey.

> **Role of the Passion Support Person (PSP)**
> **Michael's Story**
>
> Our journey continues as Michael finds his rewards in the role of what we called a "passion support person," or PSP. After arriving in Seville, Spain, Michael's perception was that our whole new world was our playground, to be discovered and enjoyed. However, after taking care of mundane tasks, such as locating a place to live, finding food, shopping, and learning the transportation system by foot and bus, what was going to be a meaningful role for him?
>
> Michael's challenge was learning how to live everyday life while I was finding and living my passion. He ques-

tioned sometimes whether he was playing second fiddle, and he wondered if his ego might shrivel. He pondered on the following questions as well: "What does it really mean to play second fiddle? Is ego really so important in the overall scheme of things or do you take the broader approach for family and community consideration?" We all take turns. In truth, our relationship roles had changed dramatically. How would we adapt? This was a question (and a challenge) that any couple traveling together will likely face throughout a long journey. We certainly did.

I soon found several PSP roles for Michael. The first was to help me find an appropriate flamenco class. Because of my lack of language, an extensive search for teachers and schools soon took on a life of its own. Since there were so many choices, the hardest part was finding a short list of alternatives. For Michael, calling with questions in limited Spanish with a totally unknown person and cultural situation at the other end was a bit intimidating. Making the arrangements and then finding our way through the maze of narrow, complicated streets was not unlike any kind of a search process. This one was also a cultural maze.

In his new role as "flamenco finder," Michael felt a sense of accomplishment each time he would walk sometimes for an hour before finally finding a well-hidden address. The teachers possessed typical Spanish vitality, grace, and courtesy. At each studio and school I would test-drive a lesson while he wandered the neighborhood and learned much more of the city and observed Spanish ways. Then with baited breath Michael would receive the summary of the first lesson. He was quite satisfied in this role, saying, "I could not have asked for more. Learning the city, the culture, more of flamenco, and meeting such interesting people and situations." He admitted that as a pure tourist, this kind of in-depth experience would not be possible. "The renewal experience, which allowed time to explore with some focus and yet being open to a host of surroundings, was priceless."

The second important PSP role was preparing meals. While I was at the studio he would often shop, prepare, and cook the evening meal. In fact, Michael found shopping to be a pleasurable experience. His feedback to me was always filled with delight. "The exotic selections are always fun," he would comment. Being financially responsible, he also found delight with a strong dollar and weak Peseta (now Euro) that made most domestic foods and wines inexpensive. Local wines, produce, fish, cheeses, breads, prepared foods, and much more were mostly delicious and cheap. Exceptions were imported cereals and certain exotics.

He learned to stay with local products, and together we sampled wonderful Spanish tortillas of eggs and potatoes, which were a totally different food from the Mexican tortilla we were accustomed to at home. He enjoyed visiting three or four shops during a week, surveying staples, meats, vegetables, breads, and desserts. He became a regular at the local green grocer who would teach him each local word for the fruits and vegetables.

Cooking was another new challenge for his homemaker PSP role. The small galley kitchen was without the usual USA amenities of microwave and four-burner range and had only limited cooking utensils. Nonetheless there wasn't very much he could not eventually accomplish with a bit of resourcefulness.

His third PSP job was finding his own way during the time when I was intensely occupied with flamenco as well as other engagements. He often said, "It was one of the few times in my life when I had so much time on my hands." I found it so interesting that for someone who needed work for contentment, he would now explore the city, which he never stopped enjoying. He would visit new neighborhoods and always share with me the interesting views, churches, cafes, and stores. He would also be the shopper for various needs, such as a small radio, which would become our indoor entertainment center, and he guided me to many fascinating shops and places.

Michael also photographed the older churches and venerable sights, trying to capture the feel of the city. Simple actions such as dropping off film and collecting finished photos were always filled with anticipation. After seeing the results he would share them again when I came home. Finding ATM machines that worked was also a small challenge (there's more about ATM and money in chapter 8). His indoor occupation was using our computer for reviewing our finances, such as investments and bank accounts, and surfing the Internet. As I look back, we found immense enjoyment and contentment in all the little things and daily tasks. Things that were taken for granted at home now had major importance. It wasn't just our roles that had reversed; our perspective on life and what we found important were also in transition.

Discovering the Hidden on the Rooftops

Something was calling me to investigate beyond the common areas of our apartment building. My innate curiosity and desire for adventure often leads me into pathways of surprise. I've been living in this building for over a week now and other than the courtyard, there wasn't much to explore or revere.

As I climb the four, tall flights of cold marble stairs, I encounter a dirty hallway filled with junk—old blankets, carts, old suitcases, a torn umbrella and three large cartons of buttons. I tried to imagine who was living up here and what these unrelated articles meant. Was I about to intrude on someone else's life? What would I say if I encountered someone unfriendly? My Spanish was rather limited so I tried to think of polite phrases—*pardonne, lo siento*. (I'm sorry.)

Suddenly, dogs bark from behind the walls of the small penthouse apartment. Alarmed, I pause and question whether or not it is wise to continue. Is the apartment connected to the hallway leading out or is it separate? My desire to know what is beyond and behind the door is stronger than my shaky disposition. Like an ocean wave, I cannot stop myself.

At the top of the stairs I encounter an imposing, large metal door with two giant bolts. I put my ear to the door and listen for other signs of human voices. There are just dogs barking on the other side of the wall. With my 5'2", 110 lb. frame, I wrestle with the bolts and struggle with the large round handle. Ah ha! Finally, it opens and I encounter eye-blinding sunlight. I'm at the top, standing on a rooftop in Seville. The concrete floor is dirty and cracked. I walk under the clothesline filled with an assortment of male and female clothes drying in the bright Andalusian sunlight. Squinting, I discern an area filled with more junk—leftover rugs, dirty laundry, old furniture, and many TV antennas. I'm disappointed at the lack of mystery or beauty.

Shrugging, I turn my back to leave until the melodious but loud sound of bells startles me. When I raise my head and focus my eyes, I am looking into something absolutely imposing and spellbinding. It is the core of the magnificent Ghiralda tower, which is world famous and the third largest cathedral in the world. From below, it is difficult to see the detail at the top. But from this vantage point, I can make out the unusual combinations of design and architecture. Every detail of the spiky spirals comes alive. The huge Moorish minaret has an out of place Christian angel on top. The cathedral is so close I feel that I can almost touch it. I find a dirty white plastic chair and place it so I can view it properly. As I sit and stare, the ringing bells make wonderful music and count down the hours. What a find! It is my own private showing.

As my eyes continue to adjust to the brightness of the day, I look around. There is more to this dirty rooftop than I imagine. Below and to the right of me is a couple sitting on nearby rooftop. This rooftop is clean and filled with plants. The couple is wearing very little except sunglasses and they occasionally embrace. I'm embarrassed to have intruded on their siesta fun.

Turning my head in another direction, I see many other rooftops filled with those unusual items that make daily lives special for others. Some are sparse; others are rich with beauty. I see the city in a new light, with rooftops filled with flowers and decorative pottery. My imagination begins to design scenarios of their lives.

As I slowly walk across the roof floor, I am amazed at what I see below. Workmen are fixing buildings, people are hanging laundry, and others are reading in the sun. The more I look, the more I am intrigued by the hills in the distance and the other asynchronous church bells ringing. There is another life up here that is hidden from the street. An amazing discovery!

Below on the street there is an ongoing flow of foot traffic leading to the cathedral. Watching unseen seems mysterious as I conjure up various scenarios about their lives. Who are they? Why are they going to the cathedral? I realize the possibilities of this unnoticed place. I can come here often to watch, learn, and think.

In life, some things lie hidden from us until we are willing to open imposing doors. My new rooftop in the old city of Seville holds discoveries just like life. Adventures come in packages of different sizes and shapes.

I settle back in my old plastic chair and gaze out at the cathedral, the clouds, and laundry blowing in the wind. Three months have passed since my discovery. The weather has changed and it is winter. It is still the best place on a cold, sunny day. I read, write, reflect and enjoy "my" cathedral. I hang laundry, watch workmen, study Spanish, and observe life.

The experience of life on a rooftop had a major significance in our daily lives, but we had to extend ourselves to find it and uncover the joys. How willing are you to explore the hidden doors and rooftops of your life? What mysteries and surprises might be waiting for you there? When was the last time you sat on a roof? Sometimes, magical moments are disguised, and we must be willing to look beyond the obvious and go deeper, or higher.

The bells are ringing three times now. Soon it will be time for my siesta.

Joys of Simple Living

> *The search for meaning that is a necessary dimension of simplifying one's life need not follow in the footsteps of theology. The quest for a simpler life is itself an infinite journey toward God, harboring the growing sense not of transcendence but of commitment to this earth in all of its—and our imperfections.*
> —Frank Levering & Wanda Urbanska, *Simple Living*

How will you adjust to a renewal lifestyle that is radically altered from your current one? Ours has changed dramatically. There is silence except for occasional sounds of my neighbor's voices—no TV blaring or phone ringing. It has been many months now without these interruptions. I feel peaceful, reflective, and creative.

Winter evenings in Seville are frosty and cold. We have no heat except a little table heater. We sit after dinner and read until bedtime. Then, I fill our hot water bottles and put on their little plaid flannel covers. We jump into bed and laugh and snuggle. Do I miss central heating?—Not really. Am I happy? Yes. Happiness is coming from the joy within. Our lives here are joyful and filled with new friends, ideas, and passion. The need for creature comforts has dissipated. I don't focus on the cold or lack of lavish furnishing. I focus on all that I have now—a loving, curious traveling companion and husband, a life filled with adventure, learning, good health, and wholesome food.

Letting go of all our "stuff" feels so liberating. Detachment becomes easy when you live a more simple life. I have no material things on which to obsess, an activity that often takes up time and space in my life. Instead, I have room to grow inside and out. The simplicity allows new ideas to emerge. It seems to give us the room to dig deeper for authenticity, more intimacy and new ideas. Every day we are being renewed and transformed.

This is something we didn't expect or plan on. Our budget dictated some of our simple living circumstances, but the letting go just happened little by little. Each time new choices present themselves, it is easier to choose the simple path. In the process of giving up our old way of living, even temporarily, we realize that something else changed too: Our definition of success. We begin to see ourselves differently. Our measures of happiness and success are changing. Achievements, money, and possessions are meaning less in this environment. In contemporary life, it is hard to find the ways to live simply and with our true values. I have the feeling that it will be the final test of our meaningful time-off.

Walking, Mindfulness, and Cultural Norms

As we strive for authenticity, we try to incorporate the concept of being mindful in our walks through the city and countryside. Mindfulness is described by experts as the ability to be present in the "here and now." It is not thinking about the past or the future but staying in the moment. It is a lot harder to accomplish than you would imagine. It requires discipline and self-awareness. During our life renewal, we devote time to explore the principles of mindfulness. It is something that carries over upon our return.

> *Mindfulness is the practice of making things real—*
> *—to see clearly. With mindfulness we become more*
> *aware of life's everyday miracles.*
> —*Joel and Michelle Levey,* Living in Balance

Being mindful can also reduce the risks of getting hurt. When you are mindful you are alert. You pay attention to details of your surroundings and people you encounter. This is very important when traveling. It is impossible to avoid all dangers, and we had our share of them. For example, every hiking experience had at least one dangerous moment, such as a sudden change in weather, a poisonous snake or insect, an unstable trail, wrong directions, even falling rocks. Because we were mindful and alert, we were more in control of our situation. In fact, the confrontations made us stronger in mind, spirit, and body. We handled each incident by problem solving using the best judgement we could muster. Fortunately, nothing serious happened.

These incidents remind me of life's many tests and that time-honored phrase "nothing ventured, nothing gained." To hide from these experiences is denying an important opportunity for growth. Michael and I have enormous trust in our abilities to find the right path or to handle dangerous situations. This has happened through practice. Each time we are tested and forced to overcome an obstacle, we gain more strength and knowledge. Confidence builds and fear retreats. However, I truly believe these developed skills are important assets for potential problems in the future as well as old age issues. In our modern world everything is too comfortable. Too many of us do not leave our armchairs, TV, or Internet for any challenges. Ultimately, it is a disservice to yourself and others you influence. You owe it to yourself to take advantage of opportunities for growth and development.

Mindfulness can also lead to greater awareness and sensitivity to cultural expectations. For example, I never saw a Spanish woman wear shorts even in the hottest weather. It isn't a cultural norm, so I conformed in order to fit in. In each country we traveled, there were subtleties that took time to understand. Some guidebooks handle the topic. However, if you pay attention to the daily routines of the locals, you will be able to fit in with ease and not stand out.

In Spain, for example, waiters never rush a meal, so you won't get a check with the same timing you would expect in the US. Ordering food, getting the check, and paying for a meal can be a vastly different cultural experience in each country. Paying attention to details will make your time-off experience less frustrating and more compatible to the current circumstances.

Women traveling alone in some countries can be open to criticism or even potential danger. Learning the rules and respecting them is most important. For instance, in Spain most women travel in pairs. Rarely, do you see them alone. In my case, I couldn't do much about my times going out alone but being aware of the code of conduct was important.

In general, a woman traveling alone out of the US should be diligent about safety. Dressing down and wearing clothes similar to the local culture helps. I got rid of my hip pack because no one in Spain uses them. I wore black instead of my usual bright yellows and red. I behaved in public the way others around me were behaving. Animated conversation and laughter are acceptable in Spain, but not so much in Japan. I asked a lot of questions of new acquaintances so I could understand more about the social norms, such as who pays for the check, are gifts expected, and what's expected when you are invited to a home? It's the little things that make a difference. In chapter 4, *Going Solo*, I address more helpful hints for traveling alone.

Leaving Again

Transitions are always difficult. We have adjusted to Spain, and now we are leaving for another destination. Will it be as much fun? Will it be harder? How will be react to a new culture? We will have to learn new money exchanges, new languages, new ways of living and making friends again. This is another challenge for us, but we are confident we will do okay. This is a good time to analyze your flexibility to adapt to many changes. You may decide that one destination is just right for you. Whatever you choose, it is okay. After all, you will be designing your own renewal and time-off experience.

Accumulation of things can happen even on a budget. Think about your desire to have mementos from your trip. What tangibles are important and how will you budget for them? Posters, jewelry, art, clothes, ceramics are all possibilities from this country. In general, we didn't accumulate much because it didn't fit with our goals for the trip, items were too expensive to send, and we couldn't carry them. However, in spite of our lofty goals, we packed a box for shipping home. I needed some practical items for future flamenco experiences, such as fans, flamenco CDs, and dance attire. Michael packed photos. At the last minute, I put a pair of flamenco shoes and skirt into my suitcase. Who knows? Maybe I'll find a dance class in Israel or Japan (I do).

The rituals of leaving begin by pulling down the little prints taped to the wall. I make a package for our friend Lucy, consisting of good wine, cheese and bread, along with the new blanket and pillow. The leftover laundry on the roof comes down. One last look over the rooftops of Seville and the Cathedral. We go to the apartment of Pepita, the house manager, to say good bye. We reach down to her 4' 11" frame to hug her. Tears are in our eyes. We promise to write. We have already said our good byes to the other families. I'm so amazed at how many friends we have made in such a short time!

I close the transom in the laundry room. I take a last look at the silly miniature, green bathtub, the dilapidated curtains in the bedroom, the simple pull out bed that we loved and slept in. I close the windows. The sounds from the courtyard cease—such silence. Never did such a small, dilapidated place bring us so much joy! We have learned, grown, and changed because of this experience. We will never be the same. The wheels on our canvas bags clatter in rhythm as we walk on the wet cobblestones past the flamenco dress shops to our taxi and on to our next adventure. I have lived one of my passions and am grateful. I wonder what passions are yet to unfold for us on the next leg of our journey?

Lessons Learned

- Living the simple life is not so difficult to achieve. The rewards carry-over in unexpected ways, such as freedom to live and explore without cumbersome possessions.

- Happiness comes from within, not from possessions.

- It's the little things you can appreciate after living in other cultures—warm water, a bath, a little heat on a cold day. These are things we often took for granted before traveling. Once you detach from possessions and a set way of doing things, you are free to explore life without being encumbered. Detaching from familiar daily life allows room for new experiences to occur.

- Handling obstacles in a foreign country requires enormous creativity, problem-solving techniques, determination, and focus. The everyday search for common things such as food, accommodations, and classes is very challenging. In the end it promotes inner strength and confidence.

Chapter 3

Changing Cultures, Changing Emotions

Emotion is the chief source of all becoming conscious. There can be no transforming of darkness into light and of apathy into movement without emotion.
—Carl Jung, *Psychological Reflections: A Jung Anthology*

Going home again and probing into one's past always stirs the head and the heart—and this leg of the journey proved that to be true. Our renewal journey was challenged in many ways when we signed up for an archeological dig. It was one of the few plans we made ahead of time.

History is one of Michael's passions, and that includes digging into the past for understanding. As mentioned earlier, going back to Michael's homeland, Israel, was also important to reconnect with his family. I was also eager to share my previous experiences in Israel with him. In 1968 my daughter was born in Jerusalem. I had lived there a year with my former husband who helped to setup Israeli TV. There was anticipation, but for me, always some apprehension entering the Middle East. Having lived through many terrorist bombings in 1968, I felt anxious leaving the safety of Spain for the unstable ground in Israel.

When planning a trip with a partner, there is always compromise. I probably wouldn't have chosen Israel if I had been on my own. However, it was extremely important to Michael. I respected his strong desire to return and hoped I could cope with the instability of the region.

Think carefully when you plan. How flexible are you to adapting to someone's strong needs? What do you need to do to help yourself deal with any anxiety?

Changing Cultures and "Digging In"

We landed at midnight at the Tel Aviv airport. We were quickly reminded of the culture shift and were somewhat unprepared. We forgot it was the Sabbath; therefore, there is no public transportation to the accommodations for the archeological dig in Ein Gedi at the Dead Sea. Negotiations with a cab driver deplete us quickly of $100 to get to our hostel. Even in the darkness, the change of terrain from Spain is most visible. The military checkpoints also remind us of the volatile area we are in.

In spite of the late hour and travel exhaustion, memories from my first visit to the Dead Sea in 1968 begin to flood me. From what I could see in the moonlight, it was still the same, with the desert, craggy mountains, the massive Dead Sea, and

Jordan across the water. There are so many mysteries of the past embedded in this part of the earth.

Our weary bodies stumble into the dark night as we locate our room at the youth hostel—bunk beds, only a trickle of tap water, and a welcome note greet us. The brilliant morning sun wakes us to a glorious pink glow over the sea. With tired eyes, we make our way to breakfast and our volunteer orientation. More cultural shocks ahead—no creamy café con leche and Spanish tostado. Instead, our hungry bodies indulge in a hearty, typical Israeli breakfast of yogurt, cheese, breads, salad, fruit, and bad coffee.

To our surprise, volunteers are from all over the world and range in age from 19-72 years. Our administrative leader Tammi is lively, funny, and energetic. She covers background information on the dig, archeological findings to date, our daily responsibilities, and details of our stay.

The melodic church bells of Seville have been replaced with a bone jarring alarm. It is 6:00 A.M. and barely daylight. With only a cup of coffee for sustenance (breakfast is at 9:00 in the field), we walk through rocky fields to the site located near an oasis. We are instructed in English to take our places for our work of the day. I'm standing in a pit about twelve feet deep with two Japanese who speak only a speck of English. My first assignment is to clean off an ancient oven dating from Roman times with a fine brush for a photo session. This lasts about four hours. UGH! My aching body groans.

Later that day, I use a pick to dig another layer into the ground to look for artifacts and remnants of the life in this village. My flamenco body isn't used to hard work in the hot, broiling sun! Our site is a small Jewish village dating to Roman times, circa 7 AD. It was apparently known for producing balsam, was not far from a major trade route, and possibly supplied perfumes to Ethiopia and the Queen of Sheba.

The work is hard and tedious. My pit companions work in the usual Japanese dedicated manner. It is a meditative day, as well, because of language difficulties. When 9:00 A.M. finally arrives we eat breakfast and then it's back to the pit. Lunch is at 1:00, which resembles breakfast. But, when you are hungry, you learn to eat what is served. Conversation is upbeat and interesting at meal times. We are impressed with our colleagues and their dedication to this hard assignment. Many have returned to this site for their fourth year.

By 4:00 P.M., I'm dusty, dirty, tired, and achy. How I long for my Spanish siesta! We hobble back to our room and manage to clean off our bodies with a few drops of water. The hostel repairman came to change the showerhead, for which we are happy.

Our evenings are sociable and educational with lectures, slides about digs, new findings, and question and answer sessions. Temporarily, we have been transported back into time. The Dead Sea scrolls were found in this area. The religious ascetic Essenes lived in tiny dwellings above our digs. There is a nearby synagogue with a famous curse in mosaic stones. "He who gives away the secret of this place is forever damned infamous." Wars have been fought, lost, and continue for this somewhat barren land.

Indeed, we are in culture shock. The easy café life of Spain has been replaced by the harsh realities of the past and ongoing struggles for a homeland. As we dig in our pits, we uncover the layers of an ancient civilization and reconstruct their lives—fire, famine, war, settling, leaving, coming back, and leaving for a final time. Findings include jewelry, a large pool (of unknown use), pots, jugs, bones, and more ovens.

The dig is interrupted midweek by a wicked sandstorm typical for this region. Wind gales blowing the sand in every orifice make it impossible to see. The storm yellows the sky and the sun resembles the moon. All those vivid descriptions in the Bible of supernatural events now seem so plausible. We stumble back to the hostel, watch through the silted and the yellow glow of the windows and wait for the storm to abate. Finally it does. We are sad to see that it has undone some of our hard work, but we are anxious to resume.

Our last evening at the dig is spent in celebration of our findings (pottery and jewelry) and our camaraderie. We now have new acquaintances from around the world. We get certificates, drink wine and dance. I don't show off my flamenco, but I manage a little Middle Eastern belly dancing.

In spite of the accomplishments from the dig, I feel immensely sad and struggle with my daily emotions. I am surprised at what is happening to me. Being in Israel forces me to think about how easy my life is in the US and how difficult it is for people to live a normal life here amidst the constant strife. How do they manage everyday to work, raise families and live life under the threat of death? I am grateful, for I have a homeland and so much freedom. This is part of the life renewal experience I had not been prepared for. However, I am glad for my deep emotional feelings, even if it isn't as lighthearted as Spain. This is all part of the journey in discovering more about myself.

Revisiting the Past—Jerusalem of Gold

> *It is dusk in Jerusalem, the Eternal, the Holy, City of Mankind, City of Peace. Heaven holds a place for this sacred city and the sun sets on the aged stones with concern and love, lighting them with pink and bronze, copper and gold. The gold that is Jerusalem. It glows with a beauty and glory of its own—a blessing on all who live and love within the comfort of her dignity and grace.*
> —Judy Goldman, *Flavor of Jerusalem*

After leaving our dig, the bus takes us through a no man's land that is hilly, dusty, and mysterious. We see occasional flocks of sheep and shepherds roaming the empty spaces. Abruptly, traffic picks up and slowly we leave the emptiness to begin our ascension to Jerusalem. We have traveled from the lowest point on earth to 3-4,000 above sea level. The city always looks magical as it shines with its prevalent pink walls of stone.

As we begin our exploration, we observe that many things have changed in new Jerusalem but not the Old City. The old dark walkways, Arab bazaars, the sweet smell of Arabic coffee, and hustle of daily life are still here. In this two square mile radius surrounded by the ancient walls there are four distinct quarters, including Moslem, Christian, Armenian, and Jewish. As you enter each quarter, you are exposed to its unique culture. These religious groups live side by side; some are tolerant, others not.

Other background on the country shows the population is 5.8 million with the Jewish population at eighty percent and Arab at twenty percent. Immigrants come from Europe, America, Africa, Asia, and Russia. The GDP per capita is $18,300. Israel is the size of Connecticut, with two-thirds being the arid Negev south. Israel is technologically advanced and exports high tech as well as diamonds and agricultural products.

We are making another adjustment having left the Dead Sea region and warmth of the desert. Our quest for deeper understanding about our youth begins. As Michael and I wander through the old walkways, I reminisce about the days with my baby girl who was born here in 1968. Who was I back then as a young mother in a strange country? How have I changed? What can I learn from coming back?

Michael recalls his youth having been born in Jerusalem in 1938. His strong memories of growing up surrounded with family makes him happy. As the days go by and we continue our daily explorations, we learn more about each other and our past. Michael radiates joy from being home. Every moment here seems to be a confirmation of who he is. His memories of places and people flood back daily. His joy is found in experiencing the polyglot, ethnic, and religions mix of the people, ancient and the new juxtaposed.

He is comfortable and at ease. I am torn between the past and present. I'm nostalgic about the past, but also nervous about the present conditions. They were volatile in 1968, but maybe I'm wiser now and value life more. The ever-present soldiers with guns intensify my fears. Michael and I have daily arguments about my insecure feelings. It is the beginning of unrest for us as a couple.

By mere chance, while in Jerusalem on King George street, I meet my oldest friend and author of *Flavor of Jerusalem* noted at the beginning of this chapter. She is my connection to the past. In 1968 we trudged through Jerusalem streets with our baby buggies and shared the highs and lows of living in a changing country. Our weekly visits are uplifting as we discuss the many events in our lives up to now, such as professions, children, hopes, and dreams for the future. I'm also reminded how nice it is to be visiting with a female. However good it is traveling with a husband, it is important to occasionally be with someone of the same sex. In this case, it is a woman who has known me for a long time.

Old friends can validate your growth and remind you of things forgotten. For me, this aspect of the journey is a vital part of my renewal year. I suddenly feel a sense of pride over past accomplishments and acknowledge the courage it has taken to step away from our work-life in the US.

In the Footsteps of Moses

One of our life renewal goals is to explore historical sights around the country and also to climb Mt. Sinai. The biblical story of Moses and the Ten Commandments has always held a special mystery for us and leads to our safari into Egypt.

After a long five-hour bus ride from Jerusalem past the Dead Sea, Solomon's mines, and the desert that Israel is making bloom through technology, we arrive in Eilat. This is Israel's answer to Miami Beach. When I visited here in 1968, there were only a few grass huts on an endless beach around the Red Sea. Rockets from Aquaba on Jordan's side would whiz by. Today, Eilat is a play land for Israel and many other countries. Joint projects with Jordan and Aquaba now exist.

We stay in a hotel with hot water, a bathtub, and a "real" swimming pool. This is the first touch of luxury since leaving the US. After a wonderful buffet breakfast, we are picked up in an ultra modern van with automatic doors, cushy seats, and absolute comfort. I can hardly believe our luck! Is this the way we will travel to Sinai? After a laborious one-hour border crossing, we enter Egypt and leave the cushy van behind. (Being flexible is one of our goals!) We are greeted warmly by our Egyptian guide and his Bedouin driver. He is a teacher for Bedouin children. The children never come to school, which is their loss and our gain. He is extremely knowledgeable and shares many insights regarding the Bedouin lifestyle. Our travel companions are a very sedate couple from Denmark (doctors) and their two lovely teenage children (The son is deaf.)

We looked aghast at the worn down old jeep we are to travel in for four days. No cushy seats to ride into the desert. Instead we must sit on two benches along each side of the jeep with a Bedouin rug covering the holes on the floor. We face our travel companions and the luggage that is piled on top and around our feet. Michael and I glance knowingly at one another with a look that says, "remember our motto, 'no whining.'"

As we drive off and our jeep bounces and sputters, we try to maintain our humor and our insides. We begin our tour around the turquoise waters of the Red Sea and the desert mountains of Sinai. All along the sea, the Egyptians are building sprawls of hotels and homes, all unfinished. Slowly we begin to leave the sea behind us and enter the mysterious land that Moses and the Jews wandered in for 40 years. I pray we don't have the same experience!

The Sinai is hard to describe. It is vast with mountains, dunes, and scattered Bedouin camps. The government built homes for them, but they refuse to live in them. They prefer the old style nomadic tents. There are natural springs, wadis, canyons, scrub, sheep, wild camels, and a few acacia trees, but not much life. Sinai is pristine and peaceful. We love every minute of our time here except the smelly jeep.

The next 4 days are spent walking through canyons, picnicking in the desert, visiting Bedouin villages, walking the dunes, and bouncing in the jeep. There are few roads in the desert except for those main roads that connect to the major tourist sites such as Dahab, Nuweiba, St. Catherine, and Sharm El Sheik. Many of the better roads were built during Israel's occupation. Our Bedouin driver is incredible at navigating the desert! Even at night he can find his way through the vast emptiness and bring us safely back. Considering the condition of the jeep, it is a biblical miracle worthy of Moses! Needless to say, when traveling in the Middle East, be prepared for some discomfort.

The highlight of the trip is the ascent of Mt. Sinai, called Moses' mountain by the Arabs. We enter the walking path through a Bedouin village and have the mountain almost to ourselves until the top. At that point, tourists from the main climbing path join us. Our thoughts of Moses and the wandering Jews consume us. We ask ourselves, "How would he get to the top without a path? How did he ever get this far with his people in this unforgiving desert climate? What was he thinking as he climbed?"

Our mundane thoughts are more like, "Can I get to the top without ruining my knees?" The climb proves to be spiritually moving and peaceful, but hard. We reach the top in time for sunset with incredible light and views of the rugged terrain. After moments of quiet reflection, my thoughts turn practical. "How will I make the descent?" At this point, I have serious doubts about my knees. However, my fears are alleviated as a lonely camel and his driver appear.

"Only $10—very good camel," says Salem, the wiry 16-year-old camel driver.

I reply quickly, "You've got a deal!"

So Zabata (the camel) and I descend Mt. Sinai under a full moon illuminating our path. This is definitely an experience I won't forget! In the meantime, Michael is looking haggard and weary two hours into the descent, so I give him my place on Zabata.

Thinking back to my life renewal goals, I am struck by how many "highs" I have already experienced. If I happened to stop now, I would be very fulfilled and renewed. This singular and extraordinary experience was more than I expected. And there is a bit of irony in this tale. The Israelis now come to Sinai during Passover time. What would Moses say after all the sacrifices to get the Israelites out of Egypt? Life is strange.

Moses was enlightened, and my spiritual awareness has expanded. It is hard not to be influenced by stories of travail and greatness. Climbing those steep and rocky steps to the top makes me aware of the many difficult steps the Israelites took for freedom. As recorded in many biblical books, Moses went to the mountain for reflection and came down with wisdom. We took this hard climb for the same reasons. A visit from God is highly unlikely, but the spirits of the past that surround us promote a sense of peace. Even in its harshness, there is an aura around the mountain. It beckons us. Simply said, "There is also the deep satisfaction of completing this difficult climb." The sheer beauty of the rugged terrain and the view at the top is an "aha" experience.

It has been a special moment in our lives that we will never forget.

> *The spiritual journey does not consist of arriving at a new destination where a person gains what he did not have, or becomes what he is not. It consists in the dissipation of one's own ignorance concerning oneself and life, and the gradual growth of that understanding which begins the spiritual awakening. The finding of God is a coming to one's self.*
> —Aldous Huxley

Winter of My Discontent

It is late February in Jerusalem. We are living with Michael's cousins. It has snowed, it is cold, and there is little heat in the apartment. My disposition has plummeted. Military warnings have been broadcast, telling civilians to stay away from public places. I can't help but feel nervous and anxious. My thoughts turn to Spain, springtime, and fiestas. I approach Michael to persuade him to return with me, but he is looking for volunteer work and is not ready to go. He continues to explore Jerusalem and Israel, and to enjoy family and friends. He is not fearful of the warnings. He is, after all, an Israeli and grew up surrounded by the pervasive threat of hostility.

With trepidation, I make my plans to return to Spain. Fortunately, I find that the old apartment is available. My departure date is set for March 3. I'm able to justify the decision by thinking that there will be a bigger rift than exists now between us if I stay. There is a lot of tension between us. Michael is angry and feels I'm abandoning him. He also wants to continue sharing. I acknowledge his feelings but am determined to follow my plan. This is a juncture we had not planned.

This dichotomy raises all kinds of questions regarding couples traveling together for a year. Disagreements and conflicting needs are bound to occur. It is important to anticipate this and discuss it before leaving. I'm able to make the decision to leave more easily because Michael and I have a strong relationship. I trust the anger will pass and we will move on. Yet, I'm fearful about going solo after being so closely connected for five months and dependent on his Spanish and Hebrew language skills. Will this have a negative impact on the rest of the journey? Will I manage on my own in a Spanish-speaking country with my limited vocabulary? Will I be lonely? How will this affect my renewal experience? Deep down, I know my doubts and fears will be answered as I depart for Spain.

Lessons Learned

- Every journey has its ups and downs. It's good to remember that strong relationships can survive the bad times. You may avoid a disaster by discussing "what ifs" in the planning stage of your trip.

- Compromise works most of the time but not all of the time. You need to listen to your heart about whether or not to follow your own course—even if it goes against the wishes of your traveling companion and/or spouse.

- You can plan for differences of opinion by discussing or writing down in your Renewal Journal your feelings about the following questions: What would you do if you disagree with a traveling companion about a destination? What agreements can you discuss before leaving on a trip that will help smooth over potential disturbances or problems? How will you cope with anger about a situation?

- Perhaps the most important lesson here is this: Return to your renewal goals whenever in doubt. It's often difficult to come to terms with decisions you make under duress. In my own case, the disagreement between Michael and me was most discomforting. Yet, we each had to dig deep inside for our own truths—mine to leave and his to stay. Renewal for me meant more sunshine, warmth and an easier, safer lifestyle. For him, it was settling in deeper into what was already familiar to him. That's why you can never give enough thought to the purpose and passion behind your renewal, its goals and objectives. Returning to our original goals was the answer to our dilemma.

Chapter 4

Going Solo

The renewal aspect of solitude is particularly helpful in relationships...Solitude of the heart creates an inner spaciousness, unhurriedness, and reflectiveness that leave room to be open to another person.
—Patricia Webb Levering, *Disciplines For Discipleship*

The alarm jolts me at 2:00 AM, though I have been awake for sometime. As I roll back a child's Mickey Mouse quilt on a child's bed, I feel a sense of dread. I shiver as I step onto the cold marble floor. It must be 40 degrees in this old house made of Jerusalem stone. It keeps the heat out in summer, but now it is winter, and I'm chilled to the bone. I have been cold like this for two months.

Rapidly, I dress and throw last minute items into my elephant of a suitcase on wheels. I spin around to see my husband's haggard face staring at me anxiously.

"Let me take you to the airport," he says.

"No" I answer curtly. "We've been through this before. The *sherut* will be here in a moment."

Not wanting to look into his eyes, I look around for any last minute items to pack. It is done. I must go now. With tugging emotions, Michael and I embrace and kiss each other good bye. Mixed feelings of doubt, anger, and fear cause me to rush out instead of taking a moment to reassure him.

The big, clunky suitcase bumps down the stairs into the cold, rainy night. The Israeli *sherut*, or taxi, is waiting. Two cheerful people inside say hello. I do not feel cheerful. I feel dreadful. What have I done? I am uneasy and question if I've made a huge mistake. Negative thoughts go through my head. "What if Michael gets hurt in a bombing attack?"

The sherut has dropped us off but I'm not ready for the forthcoming, intimidating experience with the Israeli airport security. "Where were you? Why did you come here? Where did you travel? Why are you leaving?" An hour of answering questions and having people picking through my luggage leaves me limp. Am I in a terrorist movie? I feel exhausted and the trip has yet to begin.

It's a long sleepless flight going through Frankfurt and then Madrid to reach Seville. I'm shaky departing the airport, and I miss my traveling companion. The lack of greeters in Seville makes me feel lonely. I try to remind myself that one important aspect of time-off is to challenge and extend oneself. However, I hadn't anticipated that my challenge would mean going to a foreign destination by myself!

Welcoming the Unknown

No doubt you are wondering why you, or anyone for that matter, should venture off alone. As you will see from my account below, it added to my growth and development in many ways. If you have never gone off alone this may be an opportunity to experiment. Going solo is another way to gain self-confidence and master fear of the unknown. Up to this point, I had depended a lot on my partner. Now my problem solving skills would be tested. It was also an opportunity to do some soul searching and to reflect on the trip thus far. Michael, too, needed some time to do whatever he wanted without my input.

If you decide to travel alone at some point, it is helpful to set up some accommodations in advance until you are more comfortable in your new surroundings. For me, setting up the apartment in advance took some of the initial anxiety out of going out alone. Also, knowing I have connections and friends at my destination eased my concerns and gave me a sense of relief. However, I had traveled alone for three weeks in Australia five years ago and didn't know anyone. Part of the fun was meeting new people by chance. There is no right or wrong way with these decisions. The important thing is to give yourself permission to try new things without fear.

How do you face your fears of the unknown? Do you look at past experiences and use them to bolster your courage? Do you do enough research ahead of time so you are confident you will manage? Everyone has a different way of dealing with anxieties that come with a new situation. For me, it was a combination of past experience and making a partial plan before leaving. I also had enough confidence that I would figure things out as they arose. However, in all honesty, there was still some trepidation. I tried to focus on the "here and now" and not project too much into the future. Here's what happened when I was determined to go it alone.

Settling In

My spirits begin to rise as I taxi through familiar streets of Seville. The signs of spring appear everywhere, and my body happily soaks in the sensuous warmth of Andalusian sun. The orange trees and bougainvillea are in full bloom. The harsh check points of Israel are replaced with laughter from outdoor cafes. I don't need to be careful as I move freely through the streets to my apartment. There are no bomb threats as I pass my market and no unfriendly security at the entrance of my apartment. Instead, my landlord hugs and greets me with *hola* and *bienvenida* when I pick up my keys to the apartment. Pepita, the building manager, has been expecting me. My first challenge is to explain in Spanish why my *marido*, or husband, is not with me. It is a mystery to her why I'm here alone.

I walk into the stark apartment and feel the loss of my dear companion. It looks austere and empty unlike the warmth that Michael and I brought to it for three months. No one has rented it since we left. The sweet memories of our time together here flood me. I open the shutters and hear the familiar voices of children in the courtyard. I unpack my suitcase and begin to put away my belongings.

I will have to create new memories in this temporary home. They will be mine alone to embrace. Going solo will be difficult—finding my way, making friends, but I suddenly feel up to the challenge. Once again, I pull out the little decorative posters that we put away in drawers when we departed in January. Now it begins to look more homey. Quickly, I immerse myself in daily activities such as shopping, unpacking, organizing, etc. I call every acquaintance. "Carmelita, *hola*! I'm back." Lucy, Flora, "*Como esta?*" I feel frantic about making plans so I won't be lonely.

As I develop a simple daily routine, my days become more reflective. Instead of trying to fill the hours with activities and people, I give in to the state of being alone. I begin to read, write, and process all that has happened up to now. I spend more time in conscious meditation. I miss Michael but know this time alone is important for my growth and development.

Being alone, I'm more mindful of everything around me. There are no lively conversations with Michael to distract my concentration. I indulge myself in spring time smells. There is an air of gaiety and lightness around me as the locals await the beginning of the festivities. I watch them prepare for the spring festivals of *Semana Santa* and *Feria*. I embrace the joy of spring—even in my alone state. I feel relaxed and glad to be away from the stresses of Israeli life.

I watch as mothers and daughters prepare for the season by trying on flamenco dresses of all colors and designs. Up to now, I have not seen so many varieties of textures displayed in stores. Some dresses are traditional red or black polka dots with a white background and ruffled bottoms. Others are more modern, sleek with conservative, solid colors or sophisticated patterns. They are all displayed with beautiful shawls to match the design.

The two important festivals are a contrast in every way. Semana Santa is described as the Holy week that leads up to Easter; whereas, Feria is all about parading, dancing, singing, eating, and fun. The main attractions of Semana Santa are the processions, which are endless and swallow up the whole city. I had great difficulty going to and from my apartment because of the crowds. Each procession is made up of members of a local church. The parade includes a solemn marching band with musicians dressed in lavish costumes including plumed hats. They play slow, heavy processional music, which is traditional for this holiday alone. After the band passes, we view the *nazarones*, or penitents (men and boys), who dress in long robes with hoods on their heads—a bit frightening as they resemble the Klu Klux Klan. They carry candles several feet in length, and the streets of the night parades are filled with the glowing candles.

The parade's "piece de resistance" consists of elaborate, baroque religious statues positioned on a platform and carried by thirty to forty-five very strong men. The men are under the extremely heavy platform, which is covered with a decorative cloth, and they emerge every few feet for a breath of air. As the Madonna statues pass, onlookers converse with them as if they were real! They compliment her beauty and ask for forgiveness. On occasion, the procession will stop under a balcony that is covered with vibrant, red cloth. At one such stop, I was surprised to see a famous flamenco singer emerge from the balcony and literally serenade the statue. I still get goose bumps just recalling it.

These are truly magical and mysterious customs. By the way, each procession ends at the famous Cathedral (described earlier) and the statues are placed inside. On Easter Sunday, worshippers come to see and revere them. This is an event and setting one doesn't forget, with the numerous gold and wooden statues surrounded by lavish flower displays.

After a week of recovery and to counter the religious fervor, the city looses its solemn tone and prepares for the gaiety of the Feria, a big city party. Seville is suddenly filled with ornately and extravagantly decorated horses and carriages. Even the horses' manes and tails are braided elaborately with colored ribbons and flowers. Prominent men and women ride in carriages and parade around the city waving at onlookers. This festival has evolved from a horse and trading show. Now it is an excuse to dance, sing, eat, drink, and to live up to its image of hedonism.

The main staging area takes place in a huge parade ground. Colorful, pastel *cassettas*, or tents, are set up that are well equipped with kitchens and bars. Inside they are decorated like an elaborate home with lace wallpaper, chandeliers, fancy tables, candles, and even a small picket fence entrance. Most women dress up in the traditional flamenco dresses, earrings, flowers, shawls and the men in short bolero jackets, black tight pants, and dramatic black sombreros. Men, women, and children parade around on foot, horses, or in carriages. It is a breathtaking sight that resembles a Hollywood set. Flamenco music pours out of the cassettas day and night and is accompanied by the stamping and twirling of men, women, and children all performing the passionate *Sevillianas*—the traditional folk dance of Seville.

As time goes on, I am confident that I made the right decision to come back to Seville. I would have missed these two extraordinary festivals and my own opportunity to dress up for the Feria.

Hiking Trails and Extending Myself

Desperate for English conversation, I stumble upon the American Women's Association, an English speaking organization which is not widely publicized. The connection came by accident through a friend of a friend. Just when I thought I knew everything about Seville, I discover that there is a wonderful organization that has an excellent networking system. Knowing about them would have made life a lot easier upon our initial arrival to Spain. Oh, well, better late than never.

The organization is designed for English-speaking expatriates, so it includes members from England as well as the US. I was also surprised to find several Spanish women who either had American spouses or had lived in the US at some point. The organization is geared to social activities but serves as a bank of information about life in Seville.

I make contact and join an energetic group of sixteen women and a few spouses for a day-long outing in the country.

The site is a Spanish villa located in Aracena, ninety minutes from Seville. We indulge in a three-hour lunch on a veranda followed by a walk through the lovely hills. The women talk freely and share their life stories. Some single women have retired here from America. How brave I think. Others have settled from England with spouses. These new connections provide a network when I need it.

My daily life begins to change now that I have made some new acquaintances. I make appointments with some of the English-speaking women for walking and sharing tapas. They introduce me to some new places I had not yet discovered. Even though I'm trying to learn Spanish, it is comforting to speak in my own language occasionally.

One very special friendship emerges, for which I am grateful to this day. The connection has taken many twists and turns to develop. It started back in October of last year when we first arrived in Spain. At one of the performances given by my flamenco teacher, Carmelita, she introduced us to a former and very famous flamenco dancer. Her father was an international star who danced in film and performed impressive works written by the writer Garcia and composer Manuel de Falla. The flamenco performing genes were passed on down to her and she became her father's protégé at a very young age. From eight years of age until her sixties, she danced primarily in the US. She retired to Spain and now paints. Her specialty is flamenco dancers.

By coincidence, she is a member of the American Women's Association and we reconnect on the day's outing. From that point on, we have coffee frequently, and I'm enthralled when she invites me to her studio to see her paintings. This leads to many fascinating conversations that are intertwined with wonderful stories of her life growing up with a famous father and other well-known gypsy performers. When she shows me many scrapbook photos, I'm in flamenco heaven!

Before leaving Spain, I ask to purchase one of her dazzling flamenco dancer sketches, which she generously sells at a much lower price than offered to the public. It is now framed and has a place of prominence in my home. It is a constant reminder of how life renewal opens us to special moments and special friends.

Some of my goals in returning to Spain are being achieved as I continue to study flamenco and Spanish. I hire a new Spanish tutor, a friend of the previous one who is currently traveling. While practicing my Spanish reading, I notice an ad for a Spanish hiking group. In my broken Spanish, I call and make contact. Directions for a meeting place are given and I frantically write them down. The gathering place is at the railroad station on Sunday. There are so many questions to ask but I couldn't get it all out in Spanish. It is frustrating not to be able to communicate well.

I arrive early and look for people dressed for hiking. The Spanish always dress up so this should be easy. Twenty minutes have passed. I am worried that I misunderstood the directions. Finally, I notice a thirty-year-old red head, female, with a green backpack who is looking around the station. I approach in broken Spanish. She acknowledges that she is waiting for the leader too. The rest of the group arrives and we board the train for a three-hour ride north to Cazalla, a place Michael and I hiked in the fall. The train ride is a delight because of my fun-loving Spanish companions. I listen and try to communicate. They laugh and try some English.

As we begin our hike, the path is very familiar. I end up proudly leading the little group. They are impressed that I know the way. The day is filled with much conversation and laughter. The Spanish never stop talking. I think of Michael, but I am glad for this day with new acquaintances and surprises. I feel proud that I had the courage to initiate this alone. I found my way and am also leading it for others.

Michael Across the World—Staying Solo

Michael admitted that the closeness during the past months was enhanced by much greater mutual dependence than normal. There were far fewer options than one normally has at home for spending time apart. We had language dependency issues, fewer friends and family, and no outside work. Then, too, the nature of exploring new surroundings required so many more joint decisions about finding places to live, places to visit, cultural activities, where or what to eat, and so on. Also, our living quarters were usually very compact, often one room which further contributed to closeness.

He reflected that part of the mutual dependence was extremely positive including enjoyment of sharing the wonders of places and people daily. In addition, it was ready communication of observations, humor and feelings, which could not be shared so easily with anyone else around—it was the warmth and companionship and having a virtual home base by having your partner along.

After my leaving for Spain, he realized that an advantage of staying solo would now be the flexibility to go and do whatever and whenever he wanted. These positives were counterweighted by lack of sharing and by feeling abandoned and left behind. "I wouldn't be sharing whatever adventures and joys Bonnie was now finding on her end nor she at my end."

His strong feelings that he needed more time in Israel couldn't be ignored, especially because he was so intent on locating some gainful work, which was an important and thus far unrealized goal for him. "In Spain my language skills were passable but insufficient I felt for conducting business. In Israel that was no excuse."

He developed some contacts such as an Israeli tomato grower and a kibbutz contact, but they did not work out.

Finally, he was asked by our friend Judy to be her driver while she traveled the arid Negev (South) to visit and write about the Bedouins, and a new Bedouin cultural center. He was elated and jumped at the opportunity. His need to be useful is most apparent in his struggle for finding meaningful work.

Another opportunity arose to work for Bridges for Peace, an organization which ran a food bank for the needy in Jerusalem. After many delays he was ready to start when his back gave out unexpectedly, and he could no longer think of lifting twenty-five kilo bags. Another disappointment he had to cope with.

However, being adaptable, he adjusted and found other interesting things to pursue. "The joy of this solo period was the total flexibility to explore Jerusalem in depth, including many excursions to the old city, seeing and feeling the history of the new city, visiting museums, attending concerts, going to fascinating Bible lectures and continuing to visit with family and friends."

Michael's goal of reconnecting with family could be done more effectively without me, as I wasn't as enthusiastic for ongoing family gatherings. For him, sharing the three-course daily mid-day meals with the family and participating in the life of his cousins made up some for being solo. He met the whole extended family at birthday celebrations and other gatherings. He even had an interesting reunion with a college classmate who had settled in Israel. Michael's overall solo experience was never boring because, as he commented, "The cosmopolitan and varied ethnic religious and professional make-up of Israel was a continuous source of wonder and amazement."

Family Reunions

A month has gone by. Michael and I have been frustrated by the lack of regular telephone contact. E-mail is not very satisfying with messages crossing each other. Our phone cards are all messed up and we are often unable to reach each other. When we do, there is a patter of unresolved issues.

In the meantime, I see an opportunity to have some special time with my daughter and sister by inviting them to visit me in Spain. My daughter and I have had such little time alone that this seems a perfect way to have some fun without other family members.

My sister and brother-in-law have been taking care of our affairs at home, and I wanted to do something special for them. I decide to invite them for a visit during the Easter holidays, after my daughter visits. There is nothing like a face to face visit to keep us more deeply connected.

The reunion with my daughter, sister, and brother-in-law is more poignant after being away so long. Sharing our experiences with them makes our journey more real to us. We throw ourselves into a sightseeing frenzy and thoroughly enjoy our roles as tour guides. Through the process, we appreciate each other more. The relationships seem deeper and more meaningful for all of us. The time alone with my daughter, Anna, is particularly special. For the first time we're without spouses and children. We stay up late, sit in cafes, and get reacquainted as adults, away from our usual, busy lives.

Reunions during a renewal can be special events. I didn't mention it previously, but Michael's son, daughter-in-law and two grandchildren came to Israel in February. We indeed were lucky to have some special time sharing the sights of Israel, as well as family connections. These reunions made up for some of time away from loved ones during our renewal year.

A Romantic Rendezvous

With the difficulty in phone and e-mail communication, Michael and I find it hard to come up with a mutually agreeable plan for a reunion and moving on. Michael comes up with a brainstorm that we meet in Barcelona after my daughter leaves. I had planned to take her to Madrid for sight seeing so it is easy to take a flight from there to meet Michael. We were entering a new phase of planning for our reunion.

I arrive at the Barcelona hotel five hours before Michael. It is late when I hear his heavy suitcase being dragged up the stairs of the hostel. Full spontaneity, kisses, embraces, and loving phrases encompass us. The first meeting is wonderful. Love survives!

The next ten days are spent in loving ways—catching up, forgiving, acknowledging, and enjoying the historic and magnificent city. Day trips to Montserrant provide a romantic backdrop and we splurge on a nice hotel. It's easy to get back in sync again. Michael detects a new independence from me that has its rewards. He doesn't have to make all the arrangements now. I am confident to take initiative to obtain train, bus, and hotel information.

More Compromising

Just when we thought we had come to an agreement, our compromising and problem solving skills are tested gain. The next steps for us are testy, as Michael isn't anxious to return to Seville where I am determined to be for several more weeks and then meet up with my sister. We come up with another plan. I'll go back for three weeks. He'll travel and explore the Costa Brava and south. We will meet in Seville when my sister arrives to celebrate Feria and Semana Santa. We are comfortable with the decision and focus our attention on the moment. All is well with Bonnie and Michael.

Moving On

The separate time has been good for us. Each of us has had time to process and be independent. We have grown personally from the experience. I am more confident of my problem-solving and communication abilities. I'm less fearful of taking risks on my own.

Coming together again is easy, and we are grateful for our loving relationship. There is new energy in our conversation and appreciation for each other. We love each other very much and that bond is there even in time of separation. Now we will return to our adventure together as well as with our separateness.

Lessons Learned

- Being alone develops inner skills and strength. It helps us know that we can be resilient no matter what happens. The sense of accomplishment that we gain will be with us always—even when we return from the renewal experience.

- There are many rewards to be gained by taking risks and meeting others in a different culture. It's exciting whenever we stretch our wings and learn to fly in entirely new and unexpected ways.

- Partners need some separation to better understand themselves and their relationship. By growing independently, we bring more to the partnership.

General Tips for Traveling Alone

Give yourself time for adjusting to being along. Realize that the time dimension is different when alone. Be focused and more mindful (present) of sights, sounds, people and nature around you.

Have a small plan or program—schedule something daily or at least occasionally. Participate in local cultural events as much as possible, such as the arts, fairs, and festivals. Bring reading and use writing materials. Or, if you are artistic, bring some sketching and painting materials.

Be open to meeting people and make the efforts to do so. Be sure to carry a map of the city. Dress down and inconspicuously, and you are less likely to attract petty thieves in small towns and villages.

Know how to say "help" or "leave me alone" in the language of the country you are in. When you are driving long distances, be sure to take many precautions, including a safe parking location, locking car doors, and a getting a local cell phone for emergencies.

Be aware of everything around you—don't daydream. Remember specific buildings, sign posts, etc. for finding your way back. Don't do a lot of touring alone when you are tired. You will get disoriented quickly. Don't be afraid of making local contacts in restaurants, on trains, etc. In most instances it is safe, and you will enjoy your travels more.

Special Tips for Women Traveling Solo

These tips are based on my past experiences traveling solo in Australia, Singapore, Malaysia, Spain, and the US. When you go out for the day, let your innkeeper or someone in the hotel know your destination. Carry a list of emergency numbers as well as numbers for your inn/hotel, etc. Ask in advance about neighborhoods you are planning to explore. And, if possible, find a companion to walk with you after a concert or evening out.

Chapter 5

Staying Connected

The most precious gift we can offer others is our presence. When mindfulness embraces those we love, they will bloom like flowers.
—Thich Nhat Hanh

*O*ne of the main frustrations while traveling is not being able to share all the discoveries and delights of day to day life with loved ones and friends back home. It is a challenge to find the ways and means to communicate often and with meaning. It is also a necessity because even when you go away for a year, you must effectively manage your personal and business affairs. If you do not, there may be little to come back to.

Plan in Advance

When planning your trip, anticipate all the possible ways you will stay connected to family and friends. We often think that everyone uses e-mail. In reality this isn't true. Many people still prefer the phone contact or letters. For example, my daughter has Internet connections and is computer literate but phone contact was the way we really kept the communication alive.

The phone can be expensive, but you need to determine the priority of keeping information flowing in spite of costs. In other words, plan for extra phone costs in the budget if you know there are family or friends who prefer this method. As described in the previous section, family reunions are also important. We hadn't planned it in our budget prior to leaving, but eliminated other side trips in lieu of seeing our family.

Michael's Experience with Staying Connected

The great capability of having e-mail connection was clearly our ability to stay in frequent touch with so many of our corresponding friends and family. While the human voice and immediate interactions can't be duplicated, the timing, ease, and low cost of connecting compensates somewhat. Michael isn't normally a very good or frequent correspondent, but he quickly learned to become one on the trip. Here is what he says about his experience with a different kind of communication:

> *I learned how to express myself much better in writing. Also, I had the advantage of attaching Bonnie's stories along the way. My son, who almost never uses a PC or e-mail, actually wrote a few times. His humor and personality came through very well and really touched us. Our*

> *daughter-in-law Sheryl wrote frequently about the happenings of our grandchildren Abby, age four, and Joshua, age one. She expressed herself so well that it was almost like conversation as she anticipated questions and commented on our stories.*

Communications were varied and unexpected. A friend who we normally hear from infrequently sent wonderful, lengthy letters covering news—but in a style that expressed emotions and spanned issues that we usually did not cover. Surprisingly, we got detailed e-mails from friends who we either don't see or hear from often, as well as from those with whom our normal communication is limited to a set pattern. Perhaps it was our adventures or distance, but we received (and possibly gave) signals and more intimate information than under normal circumstances. Maybe it was more akin to the intensely personal conversation one can share with a stranger on an airplane.

Nitty-Gritty Connections

We would be remiss if we didn't mention our weekly contact with banks, stockbrokers, and colleagues who handle our professional lives throughout the trip. However, in accordance with Murphy's Law of Travel, be prepared for things to go wrong. E-mail wasn't always so readily available as in our Seville apartment. Every new location had its communication difficulties. We found: wrong adapters, hostels with no phones, and phone lines through switchboards, which made it impossible to get a connection out. While we were challenged in many instances, perseverance and creativity won out. In Germany, for example, when Internet cafes were unavailable, a professor offered his office. In Japan, a software dealer let us use his Internet line for access. Mostly it was very convenient to find an Internet cafe, which were amazingly prevalent and low-cost. A side benefit enabled us a view of local cyber culture.

Work Connections

The Internet also made it possible for me to write two stories for magazines while on the road. I started one article in Switzerland and finished it in Thailand. Keeping business contacts on the trip was made possible and served an essential role. Many of our trip highlights were e-mailed to clients and professional colleagues. This contact enabled an easier re-entry to the professional world and work (See details in chapter 10, Re-entry Blues and Renewal).

Money Connections

The love of money might be the root of all evil, but cash is still king worldwide and easily beats traveler's checks and home bank checks or other instruments. The only exception might be plastic. But you can't pay the rent or many other expenses with plastic.

Our experience, corroborated by travel writers and travelers generally, is that ATM's are the best source for cash—even with bank fee charges. The fees cost much less than paying for traveler's checks, not to mention the need for a passport and the time spent at banks. US checks were mostly out of the question due to time needed for transactions and currency conversion issues.

We used ATM's almost exclusively for cash in most countries, the exception being Japan where they are sparse. Each country had a few small challenges. In Spain, for instance, we found that only selected ATM's belonging to certain National banks would work for our bank card. The ones in other countries were more universal.

Michael's Internet Accounting and Mishaps

Quite some time was spent in necessary communications via phone and on the Internet in this brave new world of information and communication. My sister, Kaylyn, learned to use the PC and got connected specifically because of our needs. She also paid most bills, received and deposited our incomes, and handled many other daily or weekly affairs. Also, we had some direct deposit and automatic payments. These did not absolve Michael from responsibility. In fact, there was often considerable uncertainty about our current accounts. What was our current Visa bill? Did Kaylyn pay any amount that was not valid? What was the state of our savings and investment account, and what did that cowboy stockbroker do now without so much as a peep?

There was a considerable need to know current finances and, inevitably, a certain amount of frustration. Clearly, things change daily and we could not anticipate everything in this fast paced world. An incident while in Switzerland provides one such example. Our tax filing estimate and extension was due. Since it required our signatures, our accountant sent the materials to our temporary Swiss address. It was via snail speed, of course, and arrived a day after we left. While we communicated via e-mail with our tax accountant, there was often a two or more day delay in responses. What's more, telephoning was expensive, and the time difference made it impractical.

When questions arose about credit card bills, it was good to have access on-line. Still, there is a timing lag on payments and deductions. It was very difficult to speak with an agent to inquire about problems and get an adjustment. When Michael saw a large deduction on our account, it was handy to get an e-mail to and from Kaylyn, but the process would take two days. We still are beholden to the diurnal and not on-line 24 hours a day.

We maintained a good-sized account balance in our bank, but still there was the ever present cash flow question. Our bank had a good web site, but there are always timing and other issues. One time in a small town in Germany, the ATM machine swallowed our card. Since we had another card we tried at another bank. It was promptly swallowed as well. What to do? We finally got some information that the bank had changed systems unbeknownst to us and thus caused the swallowing. We had to wait for the right persons the next day to explain our predicament and get our cards back.

Our investments required some looking after. Before we left, Michael gave two brokers the management of our accounts—one at Merrill Lynch the other at Paine Webber. This spread risk (he thought) and gave us a degree of freedom. Each company had secure web sites which could download holdings instantly and which Michael organized into spreadsheets.

Our funds were doing splendidly until March 2000 when Michael looked at the larger account and realized that it had massively changed in character. It had mostly new names, which we did not recognize—names such as Conextant, Digital Lightwave, Emulex, Globix, Teligent, Terayon, Xilinx. What to do? The account summary, which he was tracking diligently, was going up dramatically, but we realized this could not last. So Michael sent E-mails to the broker with general suggestions. He did nothing and the short of it is that eventually what came up fast went down fast. Michael says, "I mention this because had I been communicating better, perhaps by phone, my concerns might have been better addressed and acted upon."

Here is the good news. Despite the various frustrations and time required versus picking up a phone for home, we had the time and very good data tools to deal reasonably with needs and the problems which arose. It was usable in the comfort of "home," as well in the social atmosphere of quite prevalent Internet cafes.

Finding Connectivity

Each location had small challenges to set up an Internet connection via the phone company. When a connection was problematic or for a short duration, such as at a hostel, we tried finding an Internet cafe. In the case of a hostel or home locale we sometimes had to call or go to the phone company to make sure cabling and modem connection were correct. This could take a day or two. Internet cafes were widely available in cities, but often unavailable in small towns. Cafes were usually inexpensive and high speed. They had very good hours and a fairly friendly atmosphere. Typically we would locate them by just walking around in the central areas or by searching the phone book. Younger foreigners and advertisements were also a good source.

Trip Planning and Arrangements Via Internet

While we were visiting an information office in Freiburg, Germany, Michael noticed an adjoining office describing the sister city of Matsuyama, Japan. Since Japan was our final destination, it seemed opportune to inquire about a home stay in Japan. We learned that an application form and letter stating our reasons for wanting to participate were required, as well as a formal approval process. Without e-mail this lengthy process would not have been possible. It took weeks, all the while traveling through southern Germany and Switzerland, to button this down. Eventually we were hooked up with an American expat who would host us. There was a sad ending to this story. She had to temporarily leave her home about the time we were in Japan, and the mountain village where we worked had no Internet connection. So we had no response to our queries and assumed the home stay was off. Sadly, we never did reconnect.

More successfully, we made arrangements for our stay in Bangkok via a web site in Australia. No big deal, you can say. But due to this excellent web site it was the first time Michael felt comfortable with making both payments and stay arrangements. There was a person who helped facilitate this. Our accommodation in Bangkok was in a very good location, and though not luxurious, it cost only $35 US, including an extensive buffet breakfast. Side benefits included the fascinating mix of Sikhs, other Indians, Asians, and Europeans staying there, as well as an outstanding health club and huge rooftop aviary filled with exotic birds. In the middle of bustling and overcrowded Bangkok this was truly a delight.

Another arrangement was facilitated for our stay in Sydney. We met a couple while on the way to the airport in Tel Aviv who had a B & B in north Sydney. We exchanged innumerable e-mails because of our changing circumstances, but eventually stayed at their wonderful place. It was a delightful homey experience, and they helped us look for longer term stays and provided us with unlimited information of all types. Our other connection in Australia was the volunteer group from Curtain University in Perth. Again, without connectivity we could not have handled all the messages, the calling expense, people's unavailability, and dealing with huge time zone differences.

Lessons Learned

We learned a lot about keeping connections with family and friends:

- Share the story writing with your partner. It's a good way to compare realities, save time, and be consistent. Use the opportunity of more writing to improve your style and communications generally.

- Take the opportunity of being away and in an exotic location to reconnect with people. If you don't hear back right away from people realize that they are leading very busy lives and not neglecting you. You have a greater need to receive and have much more time available than they do.

- Stay in touch with work associates and clients. It will pay off later. Take the opportunity to acquaint them with your non-working side.

- Don't rely on your computer address book alone. Have a back up. I carried a miniature address book that had every important phone, address, and e-mail information, including birthdays and special occasions.

- Don't be afraid to ask for help when you need an Internet connection. Make sure you understand all the rules on your international phone card. Have back up plans when they don't work.

- Consider ways to meet family members or friends during some part of your trip. Photos say more than words. Find ways to download or mail special photos to family and friends.

General Accounting Tips

Pay as many bills as possible through checking account automatic withdrawal.

If you don't have home administration, have bill payment capability for everything.

For each financial institution have web site, user ID, and password written down. Also have e-mail and telephone number available for technical and management support. Michael kept a little notepad with all these in his pocket. Have regular incomes deposited automatically to your accounts.

Track all accounts regularly - checking, visa, business or other incomes, financial institutions (savings, investments).

If questions arise act promptly.

Keep an extra bank debit or credit cards in case of losing one. It takes a long time to replace lost cards.

Don't forget quarterly and annual taxes. Stay in touch with your tax accountant. Filing an extension may be advisable because all your records are at home.

Chapter 6

Changing Course

Any path is only a path, and there is no affront, to oneself or to others, in dropping it if that is what your heart tells you. . . Look at every path closely and deliberately. Try it as many times as you think necessary. Then ask yourself and yourself alone one question. Does this path have a heart. If the path does, it is good. If not, it is of no use."
—don Juan via Carlos Castenada

The joy of our trip is that there are opportunities to go wherever we want to and, more or less, when we want to—subject to budget constraints. There is a plan but we are not beholden to it. What a difference this makes! On a whim, we can take a plane, train or bus and explore as we feel like. No serious time schedules to adhere to; there are only some longer commitments. This concept opens our minds and provides a sense of total freedom.

Michael and I agree that Israel has provided the beginnings of revisiting the past but we aren't done yet. We have discussed the possibility of detouring to pursue family history, and we may never have the opportunity again. Now is the time to do it. As we get off the plane in Frankfurt (our connecting route for Australia), we decide to change course. We board a train and continue on the path of uncovering family roots. The excitement builds as we let ourselves go off on to a new path.

Spiritual Quest

It soon becomes apparent that this phase of our renewal is taking on aspects of a spiritual quest. For us, visiting Germany means facing painful historical events. This is something we never fully acknowledged until now. Michael and his family were deeply affected by the holocaust, and there are unresolved issues. Do we have the courage to face them and deal with them? Will we run away from them? Will there be some resolution? These are questions we think about as we get closer to our destination.

Our train takes us from Frankfurt to Freiburg where Michael's mother, Frances, spent her childhood. From there, we can visit the little town of Sulzburg where she and her brother, Hugo, were born. Since being married to Michael I have heard about Uncle Hugo—eccentric, creative, artistic, and a world traveler. He left Germany in 1926 for Iran, Turkey, and then India. He returned to Germany in 1965.

The quest also includes understanding more about the behavior of deceased relatives. In this case, it is Uncle Hugo's actions that leave many unanswered questions. He took his life's savings to help rebuild the synagogue that was destroyed by the Nazis. We are most curious about the latter, as there are no Jews remaining in Sulzburg. Why would he do that? This is a question that has been perplexing us for years.

Another Cultural Adjustment

We are excited like two children as we spontaneously detour off the path and into another. The train ride is a reminder that we have again entered another culture. Serious businessmen with newspapers have replaced the noisy, smoke-filled trains of Spain. It is eerily quiet. We enter the dining car and have our first taste of hearty German soups and bread.

It is May and springtime in the Black Forest. We arrive in Freiburg where there are hundreds of bicycles parked at the station. This is a student town that takes biking seriously. We have some difficulty dragging our suitcases through the bumpy cobblestone streets. Our little hotel is situated among endless blooming horsechestnut trees. My allergies immediately go on the defense.

Getting Closer to our Destination

Freiburg, an old and historic city, is a crossroad and rail center. Now, it is alive with the springtime beauty of rhododendrons, wisterias, and azaleas. Most of the city was destroyed during WWII. The famous heavy and somewhat foreboding cathedral remains intact. Some of the few, old buildings, dating back to 1700's, have been restored to give the central city an older feel. Cleanliness goes without saying— you can eat off of the streets. We are also near the Rhine River and close to the borders with France and Switzerland, which is perfect for traveling.

Part of the quest is entering the past through the present surroundings. We try to imagine Michael's mother, Frances, and her girlhood life here as she attended school and participated in the local culture. We climb to the highest point of the village so we can get an overview. We know how much she loved nature. We see miles of green forests which greatly influenced her. We try not to talk about the Germany of the past and attempt to stay in the present by slowly taking in our new surroundings by watching people, investigating shops, and sitting in cafes. After all, we are here to see and understand and not to judge.

We are slowly getting more comfortable in this new culture and Michael's fluent German helps make it incredibly easy to get around. Our first human contact (other than in the hotel) is surprisingly open and warm. We are searching for an Internet cafe and are hopelessly lost. A German professor from the nearby university observes our dilemma and stops to help us. This is not the unfriendly, stuffy Germany I have heard about.

Practical Decisions

Even on a spiritual quest you have to be prudent, discuss budgets, and find out how to get around. In this region of the Black Forest public transportation to the little towns and forests is not readily available. We pour over our budget and decide we can afford a car for a short time. It is strange experience to drive again after so many months of using public transportation. The Germans are very organized and make travel easy. There are signs everywhere and more information than one can possibly digest.

We feel spiritually motivated as the spectacular weather continues, and we fully enjoy the endless terrain of lush forests, hills, and mountains. We understand more clearly Frances' love for the woods. She grew up in a world of nature.

Arrival Point

As we get to our destination, Sulzburg, we have the eerie feeling that we are entering the past. The narrow road takes us through an even narrower arched stone entrance with adjoining ancient walls. The storybook main street is homey and quaint—like time has stood still. Our old family photos remind us that the old German style homes are exactly what Sulzburg looked like when Frances lived here in the early 1900's. We think we recognize the house. We are somewhat amazed! Where do we start? We are excited and apprehensive. Our emotions are very much in the forefront.

Finding Our Way Again

The spiritual quest takes detours as we begin to ask questions about the location of the synagogue. The tourist office is closed. The town information phone line gives us confusing directions. We start off to find it through the little charming streets behind Main Street. With our hearts pounding, we finally see the image of Torah scrolls on the top of a tall concrete building. After so many years of imagining this moment, we are most disappointed to find out the synagogue is closed. We stand on our toes and peer through the glass windows hoping for a glimpse inside. We walk around it and stand very quietly looking at it. In spite of our frustration, it is a moment of triumph. The synagogue exists! Something of the past that was destroyed in hatred has been reconstructed with love and patience.

Disappointments and Problem Solving

We don't know what to do next, so we slowly wind our way to a little cafe down the street that is located beside a stream. It is quiet with few patrons. We sit and mindlessly eat. Our thoughts are still with our ancestors.

Hours later we finally find out that the synagogue is only open twice a month. It will be open on the coming Sunday. It is now Thursday. We have so many unanswered questions that we agree that we must return. In the meantime, we get directions to the Jewish cemetery; one of the few still left in Germany. It is located directly in the hillside of the forest. What a peaceful setting for a past full of turmoil! The arched entrance inscribed with Hebrew letters is immediately recognizable. It was designed by Uncle Hugo, and we have seen pictures of it. His presence is all around us.

Dealing with Emotions

With trepidation, we begin to explore Michael's buried Jewish ancestors. It is hard to see the names, as the head stones are in ill repair and very old. We see remains of some past desecration—yellow and red paint splattered on the stones. We are startled when we find a loving dedication to Michael's family that includes his mother's name. Carefully, we clean up the area and pull the weeds surrounding it. Moments later we find the burial stone of his grandfather, then another relative, and another until we are surrounded by the Bloch family. We place a pebble on their burial site head stone in memory (a Jewish tradition). Someone has come, seen, honored, and learned. Maybe there will be some closure about the past for us now.

With tears streaming, we are torn with feelings of comfort and sadness. As we leave, our eyes fix on a stone memorial with names of all the Jews in Sulzburg who were sent to Auschwitz. It is a small apology for all the lives.

We are an emotional wreck (as I am writing this) and need to find a way to calm down. We make a plan to drive to a nearby town for the night. We are silent as we drive. I think about the contrast of our beautiful physical surroundings with the ugliness of past deeds. It is hard for us to imagine what was like for Frances to leave this quaint and peaceful home and start a life in the 1930's in a strange and difficult country—Israel.

Seeking Answers

In our quest for information, we discover that the Jews had been accepted in this region and lived side by side with the Christians since the 1400's. Evidently, the Duke who reigned then invited the Jews to Baden State and they were welcomed in the region until Hitler. Now there are no Jews. The next three days are spent walking in the mountains and hills. It is a way to relieve some of the painful feelings. Nature helps us to heal. We also feel closer to Frances. She loved walking these hills.

Success

Sunday arrives, and we are back in Sulzburg. The synagogue is indeed open and once inside we see the work of caring people. The golden columns and blue wall decorations are exquisite. The perimeters are stocked with old photos of the region—other destroyed synagogues. Again, my emotions are over the top. We sit inside, think, and are so grateful for Uncle Hugo's foresight. At one time, we thought he was crazy to spend his savings for rebuilding this sanctuary when there are no Jews to pray in it. But, to our surprise, the guest book tells us something else. In spite of the rigid visiting hours, there is a record number (2,000) visitors from all over the world to visit, learn, and pay respects. Judging by the inspiring notes in the register, it has a deep purpose for visitors. School children also learn about the past, and music concerts are held here regularly.

Our quest takes twists and turns as we are invited to meet the town historian who is also responsible for museum and cultural events that help to educate others about the early life of this town. We hear stories, read historical accounts, and find out more about the life of the family. Even in the post office we are reminded of Hugo. One of his paintings hangs proudly on the wall.

Dealing with Pain

To our surprise, we cannot part with this town. We find bed and breakfast lodging located on a hillside, three blocks from the synagogue. We walk, eat, meet people, and let our emotions and thoughts wander. It is hard to let go of anger and pain from the past. We are trying hard to deal with it. We believe in a better and more peaceful future. For our children and us, we must never forget, but we must try to put the past behind.

Time to Move On

The extra time spent in the town has been healing. We are filled with stories to tell and want to share them with someone in the family besides via e-mail. The quest isn't quite over, and serendipity steps in again. Cousin George and Deborah live only hours away in Bern, Switzerland. We are invited to stay with them. It is an opportunity to see Switzerland and gain some closure on our many and varied experiences in Germany.

Our quest for more understanding and answers has definitely been accomplished. For us, going off the path to uncover the past has been somewhat painful but a rewarding experience. In learning about the past we are more able to understand ourselves and the world we live in. We prepare to leave in good spirits and with some resolution. We look forward to staying with relatives in Switzerland.

Lessons Learned

- Digging into the past can help resolve personal issues.

- Going off course can bring many surprises.

- Opening yourself to painful experiences can ease the pain.

Questionnaire

1. What are some unresolved issues for you stemming from the past?

2. What do you know about your family roots?

3. How can your identity be made clearer by exploring family history?

4. What fears do you have about exploring the past?

5. When was the last time you changed a plan and were spontaneous?

6. What keeps you from being spontaneous in your life now?

Chapter 7

Taking a Vacation From Your Time-off

The spiritual journey is individual, highly personal. It can't be organized or regulated. It isn't true that everybody should follow one path. Listen to your own truth.
—Baba Ram Dass

*O*ur American culture emphasizes hard work, productivity, and sacrifice. Even during our renewal, we are aware that these strong principles can overshadow our instincts and alter our travel decisions. Yet, it is hard to get rid of long held serious goals completely because they are ingrained from birth. We have been practicing them throughout our lives.

Are we being irresponsible by following our desires? So, keeping that in mind, our decision to goof off was not exactly easy.

At this juncture, we decided to take a "vacation from our renewal." You may be thinking what some of our friends were saying—"Aren't you already on a vacation?" In truth, the reply is "No, we haven't been on one." The last eight months have been filled with archeology, flamenco, Spanish study, writing, uncovering family roots, and some difficult travel and adjustments. A renewal is time-off with some purpose. It is about active engagements and time for thinking seriously about one's past and future life. Time has been spent contemplating our "callings," and our careers. Where will we live and what will we do next? Up to now, we have been reading serious books, taking classes, working hard at making future arrangements, trying to find volunteer work, and even writing. (I wrote an article for Transitions Abroad, July/August and an Internet article.)

But now we need a vacation! A vacation from renewal is about goofing off, having no goals, hiking, swimming, reading fiction, and having no serious thoughts. For now, we want to enjoy and take in the beauty of spring. We are tired from all the heavy emotions of Israel and Germany. So, come along with us and enjoy the ride of vacationing and "goofing off" in Switzerland.

The Travelogue and Vacation Begins

As the train arrives in Bern, Switzerland, Cousin Deborah is there to pick us up. We drive through Bern and then to the neighboring town of Koonz. George and Deborah live in a modern condo close to a forest. It is noticeable that many trees have fallen. A hundred mile per hour windstorm destroyed hundreds of trees throughout Europe earlier in the year.

George is a cousin related to the maternal side of Michael's family. George is the genius of the family—a Ph.D. in Physics who at the age of forty began studying to be a medical doctor. He has lived in Canada and Israel, but his roots are in Zurich. He is now helping transform the Swiss medical education system. Some of his innovations include computer programs and expert systems for medical training accessed by all involved. He lectures all over the world on medical education. He is a walking encyclopedia, and we enjoyed conversations from A to Z. He also makes a fabulous risotto.

Being Taken Care Of

We realize the extent of our emotional exhaustion once we settle into George and Deborah's home. We are fed and cared for generously and begin a wonderful week-long stay. Michael and George are busy going over the family tree and discussing the visit to Germany. I do laundry in a real washing machine—a first since leaving Spain (And as you may recall, a vast improvement over the machine that ate our clothes). What luxury!

Switzerland holds many visual delights—endless mountains, lakes, and trees. We are escorted to many places of beauty, and we see the Alps from the ground for the first time! We hike along Lake Briensee and eat lunch on a hotel veranda with a waterfall on one side and the lake and mountains on the other. Then we board a funicular down and catch a boat ride back across the lake. Not bad for our first day in Switzerland.

Surprise Connections

We are invited to spend a day in Zurich with George's mother, Friedel. She is eighty-nine years old and we have trouble keeping up with her. She meets us at the train station wearing a lovely turquoise knit suit and white hat. With her dancing blue eyes she invites us to have a little drink to first get acquainted. She has a full day planned for us—walking for two hours, a boat ride on Lake Zurich, lunch outside in a café, a siesta at her home, and then dinner on her terrace which overlooks the city and lake.

Friedel's stories are the best! She gave us special insights into family life and historical Zurich. She and her husband (no longer alive) were both medical doctors. In fact, she gave up her practice only four years ago. Her war stories told us what it was like to be in a city where all the men are gone. A successful career and interesting life included living with Michael's mom for a year. She even knew Michael's grandparents, so the family stories continued.

The great sadness in Friedel's life is her younger son, Peter, who perished while saving the life of a stranger at the beach in Tel Aviv. The stranger was saved but the undertow took Peter's life. Ironically, Peter designed the unique artistic tent cover over the ancient synagogue near the archeological site where we were working in Ein Gedi, Israel. The universe holds many surprising connections.

Reconnecting with Friends from Spain

We are also lucky to spend a day with Ray, the fiancé of my flamenco teacher. We met him earlier in Seville at Christmas time and again during Feria when he was visiting Carmelita. He is a charming 32-year-old civil engineer. Hopefully, he will join Carmelita soon in Spain and get married. He gave us a tour of some of the highest mountains in Switzerland including the Eiger, Munch, and Jungrfrau. The tour includes taking a train to the Jungfraujoch (13,500'), and on the way we hike up a mountainside filled with alpine flowers and snow. I sing Julie Andrew's song "The hills are alive with the sound of music" and Michael sings "Edelweiss." Our final train ride to the top to see the Jungfrau and surrounding mountains is disappointing. The visibility is zero as it starts to snow. We do see an incredible ice palace and the research station and appreciate the engineering feat of the trains and tunnels. Needless to say, being with family and friends enhances our trip immensely. We needed these connections again.

On Swiss Life

While English is quite prevalent in Switzerland, Michael's language skills help in many ways, such as getting information and talking with strangers on trains, buses, etc. The Swiss appeared really emotionally controlled and a little robotic at times. Being timely and clean seems a first priority. There's not much nightlife, but I do find a flamenco class in Bern.

The Swiss ride bikes everywhere, and pollution is not an issue. We hike a lot to work off the chocolate and bread we eat daily, which are simply marvelous! How lucky we have gone off course and also on a vacation!

The Magic of Locarno

After leaving Bern and prior to leaving for Australia, we decide on a little Italian/Swiss experience. We love riding the trains in Europe, and so we take the train to Lucarno/Lugano area. Trains are easy, efficient, inexpensive, and allow the rider take in the beauty of the land. Our train winds through many miles of the Alps range. Along the way we see steep hillsides, valleys with grazing cows, and numerous villages and vineyards. As we get closer to Italy, we wind through lovely valleys that eventually change to a dryer, Mediterranean type terrain dotted with palm trees. The Swiss houses of the north have now been replaced by white stucco homes with red tiled roofs.

We fall in love with Locarno and find an inexpensive furnished one-bedroom apartment overlooking Lake Maggiore. The apartment has a swimming pool, sauna, fully equipped kitchen, balcony, and is surrounded by huge fir trees. A brook babbles below our window. For all this beauty and convenience, we pay just US $50 a night. We have mountains and hiking trails galore, biking trails, good Italian/Swiss food, friendly people, and some nightlife. Our landlady leaves cut roses on our doorstep daily. It's as if we're living in a beautiful dream.

Delights in Following Your Instincts

Because we had no expectations or plans to be in Switzerland beforehand, we are completely taken back by the total experience and natural beauty. We feel like we have been given an unexpected gift, and it has all happened because we followed our heart's desire and took the initiative to continue exploring.

We arrange to stay in Locarno an extra two weeks because there is so much to see and do here. The rent is economical (though Switzerland is not), but we eat in and don't buy things. The weather has been cloudy and rainy except for our first two days, so we rationalize that we can use some sunshine, which is promised for next week. One of our hikes takes us first by bus on a tortuous road through a forest ending in a tiny village very high up. Then for three hours we hike through fantastic high country, waterfalls, ancient slate and stone house villages, gardens full of spring flowers, wild flowers, many ups and downs, and trails filled with rocks and tree roots. Further down, we see a raging river for quite a distance.

We pack our lunch, but along the way in the villages, there are also small restaurants with welcome refreshments. We catch another bus back, totally exhausted with hurting knees and bodies, but in good spirit. It is worth it. Today we realize that we might not be able to do these things forever. In fact, this may be one of the reasons for planning your renewal now, as opposed to later.

Leaving Paradise and Rejoining the Real World

It is hard for us to decide that this good life must come to an end. We are so comfortable that we could easily stay here longer. But our American habits remind us to move on to accomplish more of our predetermined renewal goals. We realize the rest of the journey is waiting for us. It is time to do some work again, and for us to be more useful. Volunteering in Australia and then Japan are next on the agenda.

We have been very happy in our little apartment in Locarno, and it will be difficult to leave behind the running brook, the massive fir trees, and singing birds outside our balcony. Equally hard will be leaving the beauty of the town and region; Lake Maggiore, and the surrounding mountains and valleys.

Our stay here has been lovelier than we can say. Everyday is a living art of beauty and ease. We have hiked the hills, biked the valleys, and swum in our pool. We have enjoyed cooking and eating long, luxurious meals on our balcony which overlooks Lake Maggiore and the surrounding mountains. We have visited all the surrounding hill towns by train, bus, and boat. We even saw the Matterhorn and Mt. Rosa from a distance on our last hike in the mountains. What an incredible thrill!

We have even had time to write, read and think. Now it is back to the real world. Our route is a train from southwest Switzerland (Ticino) across the Alps through the Gothard pass and on to Basle and Frankfurt. Then we take a flight from Frankfurt to Bangkok and then on to Sydney.

Lessons Learned

- It is important to know when to stop and reevaluate the situation.

- Be honest with yourself and your needs.

- Goofing off is okay—even on a sabbatical.

Questionnaire

1. When was the last time you took a real vacation?

2. When was the last time you gave yourself permission to goof off for some days or weeks?

3. Are you in touch with your emotional needs for rest and relaxation and do you act on it?

Chapter 8

Being Useful and Volunteering Down Under

> *You must understand the whole of life, not just one little part of it. That is why you must read, that is why you must look at the skies, that is why you must sing and dance, and write poems, and suffer, and understand, for all that is life.*
> —J.Krishnamurti

*W*e had no idea what to expect when we bought our blue booklet filled with hundreds of volunteer listings. To our surprise, there were a number which peaked our interest. Below are two of the WWOOFer (Willing Worker On Organic Farms) want ads we gleaned. You, too, might be looking at these many job opportunities if you decide to volunteer. This ad promised the following:

Beringarra Station. 360,000 acres of pristine outback containing 75 Km of river country. Running 12,000 sheep approx. 800km north of Perth. Work required: mustering, fencing, windmill repairs, maintenance. Accom. for 4 people in our home with meals to suit. No children. Negotiable.

Udialla Springs. We are a small property bounded by the Fitsroy River in the West Kimberley. Emu farm with 40 young birds and a Marremma dog to guard them. Interests are sustainable agriculture, agro-foresty and conversion to organics. In the Wet season, we grow mixed pasture and forage and maintain a veg garden in the Dry (winter) River nearby for swimming and fishing (not TOO many crocodiles), walking among paperbarks, springs and river. Tough country but you'll love it. Occasional camel treks pass along the river. Please plan to stay a least a week. Up to 4 people indoors, in c/van or byo. Mixed diet as family.

Finding Volunteer Opportunities

Prior to leaving home, we investigated many volunteer sites. We found out that many of them want you to pay for a program, such as our volunteer archeological experience in Israel or for room and board. There are a number who charge a small fee and you work in exchange for room and board. Sifting through the sites and locating something you can and want to do is an arduous task. You also want the program to have a good reputation and be reliable.

We were very light hearted in our pursuit and didn't do any real investigation or checking on the options. However, since our trip, we located several chat sites that can often answer some questions you may have in the destination country such as VirtualTourist.com. There are resources noted at the back of this chapter and the next that will help as well. In general, we recommend that you ask for a name of a reference from the volunteer group who has taken the trip. First hand information is often the best.

You can also tell a lot from a phone conversation or meeting hosts in advance of a situation. In our third volunteer assignment in Australia, the woman asked us a lot of good questions and we were able to get valuable information from her. Her phone demeanor assured us of her reliability. We were right. As you will hear through the commentary in this chapter, we made some contact through our network of friends that lead to a Curtain University Program. Perseverance, networking, and telling lots of people your goals are useful tools in locating a volunteer group.

How Ready Are You to Volunteer?

In the next chapter you will hear about another volunteer and service experience. In this case, we would have done better to read between the lines and learn the Japanese interpretations for simple words like lodgings and meals. Even though we contacted a reliable group (Volunteers for Peace) and asked questions, there were many surprise situations to which we had to adapt.

Finding Your Volunteer Quotient

Here are some questions you may want to consider before you take on volunteering.

- Have you ever done volunteer work? If so, what was good about the experience?

- If not, what opportunities could you take advantage of now?

- If you are planning a volunteer job abroad, what physical considerations/limitations do you need to consider?

- Are you adaptable enough to live and work with others in another culture?

- What fears do you have about working and living with strangers?

- What information do you need in order to alleviate any major concerns?

- What interests do you want to pursue that volunteering can accomplish?

- What are the advantages for you to volunteer instead of being a tourist?

Volunteer Goals

Our original goal was to find volunteer work with an Aborigine community. My previous work trips brought me to Australia seven times over the past ten years. During those business trips, I also managed a walkabout and traveled extensively into the outback. It was when I traveled to Darwin and Kakadu in the North, and Ayers Rock in the red center, that I became very interested in the Aborigine culture. My dream has been to do something useful for the Aborigines which is a dying culture.

Up to our arrival in Australia, attempts at locating an Aborigine volunteer situation have failed. We got some contacts through an acquaintance in Spain and a friend in Israel, but pinning something down for the time we have available in Australia just hasn't worked out. Even searches on the Internet were of no help.

Our next best option, we figure, is to join the Willing Workers on Organic Farms, an organization we did locate on the web. (www.wwoof.org). They set up work in exchange for accommodation and food, and enable meeting and living with locals and seeing some of the outback. WWOOF has listings of farms and small businesses all over Australia and other countries. You join the organization for A$40, get a book of names and descriptions, and make the phone calls yourself.

Based on the list of descriptions, it is a good thing we are rested now. Volunteering may be tougher than we thought. However, our strong need to be useful encourages us to "Just do it!"

Crossing Continents and Cultures

Here are some of the steps leading up to and preceding our work experience. After crossing the Pacific we had a four-day stopover in Bangkok, our connecting city before continuing to Sydney, Australia. We were badly in need of some replacement clothing and essentials, and Bangkok is the cheapest shopping city around. The contrast from the cool, serene mountains of Switzerland to the hot, muggy heat of Thailand hit us in the face. We are bombarded with noise, pollution, and general chaos. But it is also exciting, and we quickly adapt to our new setting.

We indulge ourselves in a Thai foot massage for a mere $5.00 an hour. I splurge on a new Thai skirt and top—

the first dress I've worn since we left the US. We feel like we have been displaced to a strange fantasyland, and we are giddy in our new surroundings. The warm Thai hospitality and beautiful temples help soothe the commotion around us.

Even though Thailand is a fascinating country and we could easily wander off to explore more, we are committed to doing volunteer work. Michael, in particular, has a strong need to find some applied work. As you know from previous chapters, some of his efforts in Spain and Israel failed to materialize. Now, we are determined to be more useful.

G'day Mate

The early morning fog lifts as our plane from Bangkok arrives in Sydney. It is mid-June and we are transported to a winter season in Australia and another culture change. Cool (60-70's F) and comfortable, sunny days have replaced the hot and muggy. Australia is the most sparsely populated country on earth—17.5 million people in an area of 3 million square miles. It has a stable government, freedom, and a democratic society. British prisoners initially settled Australia but it now has many Asians and other ethnic groups. It is known for farming, wool production and mining.

As our airport shuttle arrives in Dover Heights, a suburb on the peninsula of Sydney, we are booked into a B & B hosted by a man we met in a taxi in Israel—more connections and warm receptions. Larry, our host, is smiling and out the door quickly to help us with our luggage, which by this time we refer to as "the elephants." He whisks us up to a lovely suite on the second floor. We even have a balcony overlooking five large palm trees and a garden. Familiar bird songs surround us and several lovely blue, red, and yellow lorikeets greet us from the balcony.

Larry shows us around what will be our new home for the next few days. It is fully equipped with a refrigerator, real coffee, homemade shortbread cookies, a walking stick, an umbrella, etc. Well, you get the picture! He quickly invites us down for some coffee and raisin toast. His art deco house is open, spacious, and decorated to a tee. The enclosed patio/eating area has windows on three sides. Fresh camellias are in a bowl. We chat for awhile and begin to relax after our long trip.

Next, Larry invites us for a walk to get to know the neighborhood, a diverse community, including many Jewish immigrants from South Africa. Our walk includes a spectacular view of the ocean, cliffs, and a small hilltop from which we can see the city of Sydney, including its famous bridge.

An offer to cook dinner for us makes me remember the warm and open hospitality of the Aussies. I also realize how much I've missed speaking English and find myself talking endlessly. Up to now, I've had to struggle with language and being understood has often been difficult. For months now, I've had either Spanish, Italian, Hebrew, German, Swiss or Thai language to deal with. Some English was usually spoken, but communication has been difficult for me. All I wanted to do now was talk in English, and Larry and I really talked that evening! There is a new sense of freedom for me in Australia as I can read signs and speak with anyone. We talked with Larry about opportunities around Sydney such as house sitting. We decide on Western Australia.

Catching Up

Before departing Sydney, the next week is catch up time for us—haircuts, calling old acquaintances, teeth cleaning and laundry. Larry has a real dryer, the first we've used in eight months. After seeing the site of the upcoming Olympics, we make travel arrangements to Perth. Perth is known as the "last frontier" because of its mix of Asian immigrants, backpackers, and large new glass office buildings housing mining companies. It is the only large city within thousands of square miles of Western Australia.

Traveling across the country is costly (A$595 per person). Ironically, a week later the fare dropped to A$299 due to a new competing airline. This tugs massively at our budget. Hopefully, our volunteer work will compensate to lower our cost of living expenses.

The Last Frontier – Western Australia

After five hours of cramped flying, we descend to what seems like the end of the earth—Perth, Western Australia. There are only one million people in a space that is four times the size of Texas. It is winter in late June but it feels a lot like California with lots of flowers blooming and mild temperatures.

We are staying at a modest hotel that is part of our fly-stay package. The city is diverse with many Asians students, miners, hikers, and also businessmen. After much walking, we locate the office where we can purchase our WWOOF booklet. The office is filled with many students and backpackers. We are definitely the oldest.

Making the Volunteer Decisions

We are excited as we carry our little blue booklet back to the hotel and begin pouring over the opportunities. We get many responses to our initial inquiries. Soon we have more work opportunities than we do time. We call a woman who has two environmentally friendly child learning centers near Perth with easy access by train. She needs painting, gardening, general maintenance, childcare, and cooking. My past experience teaching in a Montessori school is an excellent reference and Michael is able to handle general maintenance. We call but she is full. She recommends her former boyfriend, Bob, who has 1.5 acres northeast of Perth. He has an existing home-based natural products business and can house two people indoors. Bob also needs a driver because of a recent driving infraction.

Our First Assignment

Bob is anxious for us to come, so we board the suburban train for our first assignment as Woofers, thirty minutes north of Perth. Bob is a real entrepreneur. In the past, he had a wheat farm, designed and built farm machinery, and has raised cattle. Now he produces an essential (aromatic) oil for sachets. He is also experimenting with worms for reducing landfills and recycling. He lost ten million dollars on his wheat farm many years ago and had other major losses but continues to pursue many opportunities. His land contains six chooks (chickens), a cat, a dog, and two sheep. This is going to be a different experience!

Because Bob can't drive, we take a taxi from the train station. His bachelor home is a brick ranch that definitely needs a woman's touch. The location is fantastic because it borders a National Park. Visions of hiking immediately go through our heads. He greets us warmly and we go shopping immediately for food supplies for the week. He pays for the food, and we share in the cooking. Our little room with soggy twin beds is manageable, but the toilet is outside. Night pit stops will be chilly. We remember our motto, "No whining." Our goals are to be useful and to have the unique experience of volunteering in a foreign country.

> *The morning chill reminds us it is winter. We start the day with breakfast without our host. He is already working in his office. We seek him out and he begins a mini training session. For the next 5 hours, in our layered clothing, we cut lavender scented impregnated wax in a cold, dirty shed.*

Then we fill a huge pot with new wax and scents, let it melt and add the ingredients. We then fill containers for another 2 hours.

The reward was a long hike in the bush, seeing beautiful plants and trees, and hearing the parrots and cockatoos.
—Excerpts from my daily diary

Bob is a lively conversationalist and, over dinner, he fascinates us about his past personal and professional experiences. We are intrigued with the outback stories of the past.

Volunteering Networks

After a few days of miscellaneous work, he has no more orders to fill, so he suggests that we work for his mother, where we will get a good meal and a better mattress. We quickly agree.

We drive South of Perth to a suburban area, near the Swan River. Bob's mom is seventy years old and more hardy than Michael and I put together. A former sheep rancher, she is strong and energetic. We help her with wrappings for sachets, gardening, cleaning windows and floors, and a variety of other jobs.

Her first meal is a gem—the best home cooked lamb we've ever had. She enjoys sharing her stories of life on the sheep farm, and boasts that she could shear three-hundred sheep a day. We believe it! The work here reminds us of gardening at home and things we would do in spring. The added bonus is we get to meet Aussies and learn more about everyday life. When you stay with people, you enter their life in a special way. They are anxious to share their life stories. We are interested, objective, and no threat to them, as we are only passing through.

Volunteering in a Paradise called Neerabup

After a few days and meals, we say our good byes and move on to our next assignment in a country setting north of Perth, with the whimsical name of Neerabup. The ten acre property is in an agricultural market garden area and under pressure from urbanization. The ad says:

> *Permaculture and native bush gardens are our focus. We have food gardens on one acre developing pathways of native plants and plan to be an "Open Garden" and teaching site. Help needed gardening, welcome some cooking. Accom for two people in our home to live as family.*

Bette picks us up at the station on a sunny, warm morning. We drive thirty minutes into the country. The acacia and other native trees are abundant. We pass horse farms, agriculture fields, and regional parks. From the highway, we enter a rocky, pot holed road that winds through a unique native garden. We are stunned by the beauty and variety of plants. When we reach the house, which is in the middle of this beautiful setting, we are even more surprised to see its unusual style. It is an ecologically designed and energy-efficient house. Water is supplied by run-off from the roofs, and the interior and exterior materials don't require paint. We take our water and resources for granted in the US. We soon learn the value of conserving in a country that has often has droughts.

Our accommodations exceed our expectations. We have a room with a separate bathroom and a huge tub. There is a glass door that opens to the gardens. Our host invites us for tea and conversation. She wants to get to know us and understand why we are volunteering. She is curious about our renewal.

Bette is a former teacher and educates us immediately regarding the principles of eco-living, also referred to as permaculture. We soon learn the ways and means of conserving energy and materials and conservative living. Their home is built so the sun heats the house in winter and trees provide shade in summer. In this dry climate, they collect water from the winter rains. They have chooks, sheep and a vegetable garden. The insides of their eco-home are built with tile and brick materials that don't require maintenance, such as South African tile floors and natural brick walls. They make a practice of using few paper goods, recycling all garbage for compost, and using water sparingly. As we listen and learn, we take in the peaceful surroundings and watch parrots and other birds go flying by. We have landed in an Australian paradise!

Bette has made a list of jobs for us, which include a lot of weeding and tidying up the huge garden. As she shows us around, she constantly educates us about the plants. We didn't expect to learn so much. This is an added bonus.

Our first job is to pull out huge South African velt grasses that have infiltrated their native bushland. They are also a fire hazard. With gusto, we begin the arduous task of shoveling to get to the roots and then pulling with all our might. Michael is ambitious and feels fulfilled with this new job. After many hours, we are told by Bette to come in for tea and a rest. Later her husband Bill arrives from his work and we prepare for dinner.

The healthy meal is accompanied with dynamic conversation. Our hosts are most knowledgeable and articulate on so many things, and we roam through topics A-Z. Bill is an entrepreneur who has built up a thriving sporting goods business. His wry humor and many interests make our conversations very lively and fun.

As the days go by, we continue to learn, work, and share. Our jobs change as we learn more about their goals for the bushland environment. They want it to be a teaching center. My marketing skills go into full throttle and together we explore the many possible opportunities with them. Before we know it, we are helping with ideas for a web site, designing a brochure, helping with a marketing plan, and teaching them to use the computer. Michael and I are glad to utilize our problem-solving skills and feel validated. We are making a difference. This is the first experience that makes us realize that it is as fulfilling to work for room and board as for pay. It is a big revelation for us.

As the days whisk by, we wonder how we got so lucky to pick this volunteering spot. Our appreciation for each party and sharing our life stories has added to this assignment. We could easily stay here for an extended time. When we have free time, Bette continues to share knowledge and teach us as we take walks through the bush. In addition, we have been welcomed by the couple's neighbors, who are also experimenting with different lifestyles such as running a vineyard. We are intrigued with all that we have learned and contemplate how we can incorporate this new knowledge into our US lifestyle.

Walk-Abouts

We take a break from our volunteer work to explore the area north of Perth, which is one of my goals. Here are miles and miles of outback filled with eucalyptus, red dirt, acacia, native Banksia, early spring wild flowers, gum trees, black boy plants, scrub, as well as emus, and kangaroos. We drive a hundred miles before we see any gas stations or houses. It is exhilarating to be in wide-open spaces without Starbucks coffee around the corner. We also experience fear of unknown eventualities, especially when we get lost. If a breakdown should occur, we are far from any service station.

We spend time in Kilbari National Park, 200 miles North of Perth. The park is known for its gorges and outdoor life (canoeing, fishing, hiking). We challenge ourselves physically by taking a strenuous hike into the river gorge and its many unmarked trails. The Indian Ocean surrounds Kilbari on the west, where we experience a different kind of wildness. The laid back Aussie style is in evidence with people enjoying the great outdoors as one of their favorite pastimes. We join a canoe trip down the river and indulge in a camel ride.

My longing for wilderness is never fully satisfied, and I could easily continue north to the Kimberly area. Michael reminds me that we are due back for more volunteer work and a speech I have promised to make for a child care task force. (This came up because of Bob's girlfriend, who is a leader in developing corporate childcare.) Reluctantly, we drive back to Perth via a town known for schooling and housing kidnapped Aborigine children until the 1970's. This has been part of a current political controversy because the government has never fully apologized for taking children away from Aborigine families.

Speaking Engagement Down Under

I had agreed to make a speech regarding work-life strategies for corporations. Now that it is time to do it, I realize I have nothing appropriate to wear. Somehow, I put together an all black outfit (blouse and slacks) with a colorful scarf, but the only shoes I have are sandals and hiking boots. Not wanting to spend money for one presentation, I realize I still have my green suede flamenco shoes with me. No one will ever know the difference so long as I walk quietly. (It's the nails on the bottom that make noise.)

Suddenly I have a panic attack. Can I still give speeches? It has been ten months since I've been in front of an audience. Will I remember the material? Will I be able to have energy and enthusiasm for what I left behind? Fortunately, like swimming, my old skills kick in, and the speech goes well. I actually enjoy it and realize that the sabbatical time can have a positive affect on my profession. This is very reaffirming at this juncture of the trip.

Laverton and The Aborigine Experience

Unexpectedly, one of our contacts for volunteer work with an established Aborigine community comes through. Through a Curtain University contact, we are able to join a group of volunteers that are part of a joint venture with the mining company in Laverton, 1,100 kilometers north east of Perth. The volunteers are trying to bring the community together by developing options for the Aborigine people. These include using a food program, recreation opportunities and various other new ideas. The Curtain students have been working with the community for a few years instituting youth programs and donating goods and time to increase the general welfare of the families living in Laverton. The mining company is flying us on a Friday, and we return on Monday. The Curtain volunteers are delighted to have us along on the excursion.

Dusty, barren, and unkempt is the best description for this tiny desert town. An elder, respected Aborigine has died recently so there is no one around and no structure to our weekend. After all this build up, it is a huge disappointment.

Our accommodations are the worst so far. We are the first people in a year to sleep in an abandoned mining camp. Spiderwebs, tin roofs, dust, and garbage greet us. No warm blankets or towel. We must buy two pathetic dishtowels to dry ourselves. There are no cooking utensils in sight, just a huge empty room which was once a cafeteria.

Our student compatriots are energetic and don't seem to mind the inconveniences. We immediately put on our best smiles on as we clean Aborigine community center latrines, a garbage filled yard, and water a dying garden. The one restaurant in town is something out of a western movie. I expect a gunfight and brawl at any minute. Our bar waitress looks like she is dressed by Belle Star, with cleavage very abundant.

What can we do but laugh! And we do laugh a lot, along with our student friends. To pass the time, we share stories and learn about their lives. One student is from Singapore, one from Malaysia, and another from Indonesia. They compliment us on our courage. We suddenly feel very proud of our adventure and realize we are giving others the courage to experiment with their lives.

We practically freeze at night because winter in the desert is cold (30-40F). But the morning sunrise on the desert makes up for the cold and my morning walk is moving as I watch families of emus in the desert. I'm also appalled at the garbage strewn in the desert. The Aborigines were nomads and used to leaving their foodstuffs behind (bones from birds, crocodiles, small animals, etc.) as they roamed the countryside. In the days before plastic and paper, that worked. But today's fast food society with plastic and coke bottles leaves a sad trail of refuse. Abandoned cars are also evident.

Unexpectedly, we meet the mining company rep who is coordinating between the university and its Aborigine project. He conducts a training program for the tribes and is a dedicated problem-solver. He spends time with us explaining the circumstances and issues with the town and the Aborigines. We also get a surprise tour of the gold mine with its huge craters, which looks like a moonscape. My earlier memories of the relatively pristine outback are massively scarred in the desert before us. We watch in awe as we see these huge craters filled with water. One benefit is their potential use as fish farms for the tribes. Some people say this is progress and helps the economy. And, yes, they are trying to reclaim some of the area and give some back to nature when they are done. Somehow, we feel, as the Aborigines do, that these scars will never heal.

Leaving Roots in Australia

We returned to Bette's and Bill's for one last week of work and learning. We realize now that we have stayed as long as our time permits. The last leg of our trip is rapidly coming upon us. It is hard to say good bye to these new friends and the Australian wilds, which we love so well.

On our last morning, Bette brings us each a small acacia sapling to plant, "So we will have roots in Australia," she says. With tears in our eyes, we dig up the red soil and put our roots firmly in, hoping they will stand strong one day. I secretly hope to return again and see them grown up with my own eyes.

Lessons Learned

Volunteering can enrich your life in many ways as it did ours by:

- Validating old skills.

- Highlighting skills you didn't previously recognize.

- Providing a way to make new friends.

- Reminding you of the value and need for work.

- Pushing you physically and mentally.

- Making you feel good about yourself and ability to adapt.

- Offering you an opportunity to integrate into another culture.

- Giving you ideas to use for your lifestyle back home.

Tips for Volunteering

The travel center where we purchased our WWOOF guidebook has other useful resources. You can find rides and part-time work posted. They also have Internet services, travel arrangements, maps, and classes. The one in Perth was located at 513 Wellington St. (08) 9321-8330.

Chapter 9

Work Camps, Rice Balls, and Bowing

All growth is a leap in the dark, a spontaneous unpremeditated act without benefit of experience.
—Henry Miller, *The Wisdom of the Heart*

Unknowingly, we have saved the hardest part of the journey and volunteer work for the end of our trip. Our volunteering and traveling in Japan required us to extend ourselves in ways we had not anticipated. We thought it was hard in Australia. It was a piece of cake compared to our Japan experience!

Stretching Ourselves to the Limits

The trials of adapting to a very different culture, extreme weather conditions, difficult communication, primitive accommodations, and unusual amounts of rice to eat, are all vividly described in this chapter. If we had known this in advance we probably would have made different choices. However, the challenge was presented to us, and we decided to "save face" and work through the physical, emotional, and intellectual demands of the work camp. If we had left early, not only would we have broken our verbal and written agreement, but also we would have let ourselves down. Pushing through hard experiences is part of the learning in our renewal year. In retrospect, it made us much stronger, adaptable, flexible, and glad for the experience. Has this made you curious enough to read our account? We hope so.

Entering a Mysterious and Ancient Land

Once again we cross Australia, this time west to east. Our round the world ticket takes us through Bangkok again with a short, two-day stop over and then on to our last destination, Japan. We were told that transportation in Japan is very expensive. And so, while in Australia, we organize a flight within Japan and purchase a rail pass. This pass is like gold and extremely convenient, plus it saves us hundreds of dollars in rail fare. It can only be purchased outside of the country. It is purchased on a weekly basis, and there are no refunds if you don't use it. The cost is approximately $145.00 per week.

Our biggest dilemma is determining how many weeks we would use the pass. Not having a clear itinerary, we are unsure. We buy a three-week pass to cover eventualities, which later we regret as we don't use all of it. If you are more sure of your timetable and destinations, it is very economical and makes sense to purchase the pass ahead of time.

Arranging Our Volunteer Work

Our goals in Japan are to volunteer, participate in home stays, and see as much of the traditional, rural life that is within our time frame and budget. Making arrangements for Japan started back in spring through the travel bureau in Freiburg, Germany (described earlier) when we made contact with home stays with its sister city of Matsuyana. Communications with a contact person has been sketchy along the way, and we have still not received the final go ahead. This should have been a red flag for us. Communication in Japan is very difficult if you aren't on a tour! It's not impossible, but it requires enormous energy and constant confirmation that you understand—and have been understood.

We turned to another alternative, The Volunteer for Peace Organization, www.vfp.org. The VFP is found worldwide and offers many opportunities to volunteer in exchange for room and board. Opportunities include archeology, rebuilding castles, restoring villages, educational work with children, etc. Initially, we applied to work in the north of Japan with learning disabled children. The program is filled up, and the only available space within our timetable is the work camp in Hoshino in the south island of Kyushu. Here is the description of the camp:

> *Volunteers for Peace Work Camp Organized together with a local group formed for this project by various groups such as forestry cooperative, local youth group, Kyushu NICE, etc. This village has got the 1st prize at the national contests for beautiful stars in the sky and for shelves of rice fields. In spite of such wonderful natural heritage, depopulation of especially youth are serious here as well as many other areas in Japan. We aim to help nature protection and to activate the area by work camps. Work: We will do various forest work such as to make wood charcoal, its oven and a hut, cutting bushes and also help to prepare, run and clean the local summer festival. There may be weekend work camps organized by Kyushu NICE also for training volunteers to work camps*

abroad. Part of Greening Asia. Goals: How to overcome depopulation and greening Asia. Bring some info.! Home stay, watching stars, exchange parties, etc. Accommodation: A lodge in the camping site! Location: Small village surrounded by mountains, about 80 km south of Fukuoka. There will be national Summit (conference) for protecting beautiful shelves of rice fields in 2000. Q: Motivation to love the village and to watch stars.

What got my attention was the last line of the description. How could we not love watching the stars? What got Michael's attention was the forest work. Could we actually do this work at our age knowing our physical limitations? Accommodations sounded okay, so we filled out the lengthy form on e-mail, which included a full-page description of "why we wanted to work in Japan." We also had to sign a separate form for the Japanese organization agreeing to a long set of rules. This was the beginning of our experience with the Japanese culture. The fee for joining VFP is US$200 each.

As I mentioned in the previous chapter, the interpretations of English words can be confusing. When the camp description said: Accommodation: "A lodge in the camping site," we assumed a wooden lodge with comfy chairs and tables, like lodgings in the West. Never make those assumptions when in Japan. The actual Japan lodge is quite different as described in the following sections.

Arrival—Fukuoka on Kyushu

We decide to avoid the travel expense and chaos of Tokyo and go directly to Fukuoka, the connecting city to our work camp. It is located a two-hour train ride in the southwest island of Kyushu. We allow ourselves four days to get over jet lag, acclimatize ourselves to Japanese culture, and learn our way around before entering a work situation. (On a side note, homeopathic pills called No Jet-Lag help my jet lag.)

We have arranged for a hotel via the Lonely Planet guidebook, which makes traveling to Japan much easier. The reservations had been made in Australia by phone. We purposely situate ourselves in lodging across from the train station, so we can make our connections to the work camp easily. (Earplugs help ease the annoyance of all-night train announcements.) We, of course, still have our elephants (suitcases), which make it more difficult to get around Japan. One reason is due to the very small hotel rooms.

Our budget hotel called the Green Hotel, which is part of a chain of business hotels, is about as big as a closet. Our suitcases barely make it in a room the size of a dime. There is not enough room for Michael and I to stand up simultaneously. I have a laughing attack. This is definitely a funny situation; Michael stands up, and I lie down on the bed. (It's like a Marx brothers routine!) The room is compact but very well designed. The Japanese are efficient users of space and it has everything we need, including a TV positioned at the foot corner of the bed, a tiny hot plate for green tea, a tiny fridge, and a miniature self-contained bathroom, but still incorporating a deep bath. (The Japanese love their baths.) Beautiful yukatas (Japanese robes) are laid out on the bed every night, along with slippers.

Our first day is spent in the train station. You can live there (and some people do)! It takes us two hours to locate the information booth. I am dizzy from the barrage of strange symbols, sounds, and advertising. We observe how little English is written or spoken. Making arrangements is going to be more of a challenge than we realize. We take in the wonderful displays of food and try a little of everything. The Japanese have plastic replicas or photos of the food, which makes it easier for us to order. We observe the varied attire of the

Japanese. We see no westerners and acknowledge the strange feeling of being a visible minority. With my blonde hair and Michael's beard we really stand out. You rarely see a Japanese man with hair on his face.

Day 2—Exploring Out of the Train Station

On day two we venture out of the train station, try out the local subway trains, and walk around this sparkling, fairly modern city. It is hot (90 F) and humid. We need to make an Internet connection and the translation for finding the location is not clear to us. We wander about without ever finding it. However, we do see our first "love hotel," which I had read about in the Lonely Planet. It is an adult hotel that is paid for by the hour. Later in the day, though, we stumble on a computer shop and a generous salesman invites us to use his computer to do our e-mail. This is all done with very little spoken English.

Eating Experiences

We lunch in a businessman's noodle shop—no women in sight. Everyone laughs when we point to a customer's food and try our first travel guide Japanese. We wander around the city, visit the parks and port, and are surprised to see many beautiful birds such as egrets, herons, and Japanese cranes. For dinner, we sample food in the little portable snack stalls on the sidewalks. Often, these food stalls are manned by a couple. They are fully self-contained with kitchen stoves and stools for sitting. They sprout up like mushrooms after dark.

We are greeted warmly by a proprietor and customers with charming smiles. A few Japanese male customers try their limited English and compliment us on our use of chopsticks. One man, a government worker whose English is quite good, stays and talks with us for two hours. At 9:00 PM, he then invites us to visit his home and meet his wife. He insists on paying for dinner and takes us home in a taxi. This hospitality continues throughout our stay in Japan. What generosity we encounter! Would we do this for a stranger at home?

Hi Ho—It's Off To Work We Go

We have done our research well and got on all the right trains to the small city town where we are to meet up with the drivers who will take us to Hoshino Village, our work camp in the mountains. We are jittery and feel like kids arriving on the first day of camp. Will they like us? Will we be able to fit in? What will they expect of us?

We arrive two hours early and roam around the city, one at a time because of our heavy luggage. Soon the waiting area is filled with Western and Asian faces, all of them with backpacks. One by one, we greet our fellow campers. We are happy to speak English with two male Germans, one Frenchman, and one Spaniard. We climb aboard the vans and are off on our camp adventure.

The river valley and mountains of Hoshino soon greet us. Lush forests, running streams, and traditional Japanese farmhouses suddenly surround us. This is the Japan we were hoping to find. The little mountain road winds around until we enter a summer camp/resort, which is to be our base.

Work Camp "Lodging"

We are shocked to see our sleeping quarters for the ten-day stay. In Japanese terms, a lodge means an empty communal bungalow fully furnished with a wooden floor. One lodge is for the women and one for the men. Before long, I discover I will be sleeping on a futon surrounded by thirteen other women, nine Japanese, three Korean and one Irish lass, in a very cramped space. There is room for four people to sleep above the floor on wooden bunk beds. Being polite, I ask permission. I think they take pity on me since after all, I'm old enough to be their mother (average age twenty). We share one bathroom. Part of the small bungalow is used for cooking. In that corner there is a sink, hot plate, and a freezer. I feel claustrophobic.

Michael is not as lucky as I am. He must use the outside toilet facilities which is a walk down a rough trail. I think he is quite ready to bolt. I reassure him things will improve. They don't. Our evening meal is on the floor of the women's bungalow. Michael's knees simply won't bend. He looks entangled in legs. We smile a lot as we eat our miso soup and rice balls. After dinner, our camp leader begins our orientation using a chart she has made. Her English is very limited, and we realize this volunteer experience will be difficult for all of us.

The chart indicates we will be rising for breakfast before 6:00AM and working most of the day. There are some spotty times off and information on other activities and events for the week. At the top of the chart it says, "Please Keep Time," which we interpret as "don't be late."

More Surprises and Dilemmas

We are also informed that the volunteers will do all the cooking in teams of three. The one puzzling question is how are we going to cook for twenty people? As the cooking teams are announced, no one tells us where the food will be purchased, what the budget is, or how we manage to produce it with two hot plates and a rice cooker. No one asks the question, and I decide not to start any trouble. My optimistic nature says we will figure it out.

Communication—Very Difficult

After going through the work schedule, we have our first Japanese lesson and then introduce ourselves in English. Following the Japanese pattern we say, "My name is Bonnie. You may call me Bonnie. I am from America." This is exactly what every Japanese person said. The VFP write-up assured us the camp will be run in English, and we are getting the picture that the English spoken here will be quite rote and not conversational. Michael and I say our good nights under the stars of Hoshino and eat the remains of a sandwich he saved from the train station. I'm grateful, as I am still very hungry. Rice balls just don't fill me up.

Day 1

Hoshino is a beautiful village nestled along a lovely river valley. We are told that the area is losing its youths to the cities for lack of work. Forests are all around, and the camp goals are to help with fostering new growth of the surrounding forest. In addition, we are to have a home stay and help prepare and participate in the summer festival.

Our forest work here includes using a scythe to cut bushes around the newly planted trees. This is fairly dangerous work with steep slopes, sharp tools, temperatures above ninety, and many bees, snakes, and mosquitoes. We start at 7:00 A.M. punctually and end around 4:00 P.M. This is a great way to lose ten pounds. As customary in Japan, the work is properly introduced starting from broad principles, i.e. global greenhouse warming. The cutting methods are well explained with drawings and a practice session.

We don't complain and work quietly alongside the Japanese who are working so hard. We want to "save face." After all, we are the default representatives of the US. We are also the elders. Our Asian volunteers (Korean and Japanese) also work diligently and never complain. They do what they are told and unlike the westerners never ask why.

Camp Cooking

It is 5:00AM and I peek through my eye shades to see Michael cutting onions on the cutting board on the stoop of our bungalow. He is making a breakfast dish of eggs, onions, potatoes and tomatoes. He is adamant about preparing something other than rice balls, a sour plum, and miso soup. He is creative considering the choice of available supplies. Each day at camp requires improvisation from the team of three who cook for the whole group. Have you ever tried to make food for twenty people using two hot plates and a rice cooker? When it is your turn, you rise at 5:00 A.M. and start cooking for the day. In addition, we can't get food supplies with which we are familiar. So, we make up recipes using vegetables supplied by local farmers, which includes tomatoes, potatoes, bok choy, and eggplant. (Michael and I can now apply for jobs as short order cooks.)

Typically, for breakfast, lunch, and dinner there is always rice, miso soup, and vegetables. If we are lucky, we can negotiate for some white bread with honey for breakfast. Bread, however, is expensive. When it is my turn to make breakfast, I negotiate successfully and make French toast. It takes me ninety minutes on one frying pan, cooking outside on the stoop.

Adjusting?

This living/working volunteer work is making us more flexible than we can describe. There are also moments when we seriously want to leave because of the frustration and lack of communication. Sleeping has also been difficult because twenty-year-olds don't go to bed early. They go out in the middle of the night to look at the falling stars, and they don't do it quietly. In contrast, we oldies need our sleep. At other times, we are grateful for this unusual cultural experience, and we know that they appreciate our presence.

Village Life

Besides the forest work, we spend a morning visiting the local elementary school. Fifty-two children come back from their vacation especially for the purpose of greeting us, singing songs, and showing off some English skills. In turn, we use broken Japanese to say our names and tell where we are from. Later on, we are placed into small groups with the children and go to classrooms to play games, learn ink painting, and try origami. It is a very special day for us in Hoshino, and we feel most welcomed.

A Japanese Home Stay

Just when we think we can't make it for another day or night, it is time for our home stay. Each camp participant is invited to stay with a family for 24 hours. We are saved! One of our Japanese camp members accompanies us to help translate. Our host couple doesn't speak any English.

We are in awe as we drive up to the lovely 100-year-old, Japanese, traditional farmhouse. It is located in the hills with a river flowing below. The couple have a pond, fish, a garden, and family shrine. This is like a scene out of a travel book. This farmer owns rice, tea, and flower fields. In addition, he inherited a mountain of trees.

After leaving our shoes outside the door, we are ushered upstairs to our own private room. What a treat! A lovely futon awaits us on the floor and there is a toilet nearby. Michael is very happy with the arrangement and our view of the mountains. Tonight we won't hear the midnight chatter of young voices. Instead we will be put to sleep with the gurgling sounds of the river. Our sleeping conditions are suddenly improved!

Soon, our male host shows us around his home. He wears what looks to me like summer P.J's. It is the more typical relaxing outfit worn after work hours by men. We "OOH" and "AHH" at the garden, the highly polished wooden floors, and the sliding doors that open to the mountains. There are no closets; only hooks for clothing. A few paintings and prayer statues are scattered throughout the three rooms. The house is simple but elegant in its natural beauty.

Dinner is served in the kitchen, which is a combination of appliances and decor that are both old and new. The table is set with about fifteen different bowls that are neatly arranged. Most of them are filled with food we've never seen. No rice balls are in sight. We sit on the cushions on the floor and begin to "chow down." Other than delicious potato salad, squash, and salads, we have no idea what we are eating, but it is wonderful. The melon served for desert is an expensive treat in Japan.

Conversation is manageable with the help of our young camp translator who picks up her vocabulary book regularly to find the right words. The evening is filled with ongoing conversation and laughter. We hear about their farm, children, and lifestyle. We show pictures of our family and soon their family album is brought out. It is amazing what we learn about each other with so little language!

The next morning we are again treated to many little delicacies for breakfast. We are now getting used to green tea instead of expresso for breakfast. We can manage the fish and vegetables as well. When you are hungry you eat what is put in front of you, which is an important lesson for us. Sometimes, I think we are very spoiled in the US. We have too many choices, and we take so much for granted.

Our male host takes us on a tour of his green and lush fields. Rice and tea fields are incredibly peaceful to view. We visit his mountain and the many cedar trees that surround it. Finally, we are taken to a temple in the hills, where we climb over two-hundred stairs. We watch silently as he goes through his prayer ceremony of honoring his ancestors. We are having a wonderful day off from the arduous task of cutting bushes.

We hate to leave, but the camp work is calling us. We feel so lucky to have had this short stay. For a brief moment, we are able to get an inside view of a Japanese family. In many ways, they are not so different from us. They have work, families, and customs. They love their children and grandchildren. They work hard, like Americans. What is different are their unique traditions and culture. It feels good to have a common connection in Japan. They have shared so much and opened their home to us. We have been so welcomed. We realize how little we do that in the US. Maybe this will be a new goal when we return home.

As we leave, our hosts tell us that they hope we will never forget them, and they praise us for our willingness to work for the village. My heartstrings are tugged when they so openly compliment us and express their gratitude. Our stay is all too brief but we rekindle our enthusiasm for returning to camp for the next phase.

Festivals, Water Balloons and Work Styles

There is new excitement at camp. There is going to be a summer festival, and our job is to help. What we will be doing has never been fully explained until we arrive at our appointed time in the town's baseball field. We are told that there are tents and a stage that need to be put up. We are also told that we should plan an entertainment at the festival. In doing these activities we find some more of the differences between Western and Japanese work styles. We anticipate brainstorming, problem solving, and discussing the best way to do the job. The Japanese, however, seem to approach it with less planning and in the way it has always been done—and maybe not the best way.

There is tension and frustration after many hours in the heat and dust, but the tents and stage are in fact standing. Next, we go inside to make "Yo Yo's." We do this by filling up balloons with water and tying them with rubber bands so they can be bounced up and down as Yo Yo's for children. These will be sold to the children at the festival.

We are feeling giddy with this child-like activity. Soon we are squirting water and playing like kids. It is a comic relief after all the previous serious work. It ends abruptly, though, when Michael makes some suggestions on how to improve the process. Again, we are reminded that we are in a culture that doesn't value creativity the way we do. There is a young woman volunteer who becomes very offended at the suggestions and soon gets up and leaves in tears. We are also upset by this turn of events and are reminded of the delicate nature of cultural differences. Michael does his best to connect with her later, but the situation is a lesson for us.

Kimonos and Green Tea Ice Cream

The time for the festival arrives. The three Koreans, an Irish gal, and myself have been loaned colorful kimonos to wear. Dressing takes about two hours. I'm intrigued as I watch my helpers with the slow and graceful process of putting my kimono and cummerbund together.

Proudly, we strut out to the festival grounds where we see large gatherings of colorfully dressed women in their festive kimonos. Michael is wearing a blue and white print Japanese jacket that ties in front. We have our pictures taken with colorful international flags and mountains in the background.

For the festival, our responsibility is to sell green tea, chocolate, and vanilla ice cream. What a hoot! Now I have another new skill to add to my resume. With gusto and smiles, we scoop up lots of ice cream and before the evening is over we are sold out. The money collected goes to the camp fund so we are proud of our contributions.

The Hokey Pokey

It's entertainment time! Very late in the week, we are informed that not only will we set up for the festival and man a sales booth, but we will perform at the festival as well. At this point, we are asked for ideas. There is an uncanny silence except for one Korean girl who recommends drumming on cans and bottles to make music. The idea is vetoed. Silence again. Somewhere deep inside me, from my Montessori teaching days, comes the song and dance, the "Hokey Pokey." Of course, the Japanese don't know it, so that is in our favor.

One of our observations about the Japanese is that they are receptive to dance and music. In fact, one evening they asked me to teach them some flamenco steps. We did, in fact, have a fun evening of stomping around our bungalow floor with hanging laundry flapping in our faces. My recollection of their enthusiasm gives me the courage to suggest such an idea.

After I sing and show them the dance, their eyes sparkle, and it is agreed that everyone will learn the song and dance. I make the suggestion that we perform it in English and Japanese and feature one of the Japanese women who is more fluent in English. As it turns out, she was the one upset about the balloon incident. The suggestion is welcomed.

Before or after dinner, I view the Japanese practicing what they called "The Hanky Panky." They take things very seriously, and this is a perfect example of working hard on any assignment they are given. It is an admirable quality.

I won't ever forget the moment we got on the stage. The stars of Hoshino are shining, and it is a sultry evening. The audience is anxiously awaiting our performance. There are some introductions; we all say our names and home countries in Japanese. Our most fluent camper, the Spaniard, makes the Japanese smile and laugh with his comments in Japanese. It sets the mood for our performance. Then the moment arrives as I step forward leading my little troupe of performers. "You put your right hand in, you put your right hand out…and you shake it all about. You do the hokey pokey and you turn yourself around. That's what it's all about."

The Japanese verse comes next and soon we are rocking and rolling in our kimonos and jackets. The Japanese are smiling and clapping. Next, I get the audience up on their feet to do a couple of verses with us. Applause follows. We are a success! We hug each other as we all descend the steps and leave the stage.

Waves of deep emotion run through Michael and I as we stand and watch the fire works which culminate a very successful day. It is a night to remember forever. I think back to the camp description: "Motivation— to love this village and to watch stars." We love this village, love the stars, and are immensely grateful we pushed ourselves to this point. We would have missed so much if we had given up because of the discomforts. This is the big lesson for us. After the discomforts come the rewards.

Moving On

We have had the farewell party and said our good byes to the village people. We have made recommendations for improvements for next year, which was difficult. (None of the Japanese campers made any suggestions.) We have exchanged e-mails and notes. The Japanese have a tradition of writing little notes to each other in special notebooks. It reminds me of when I graduated from high school and we wrote in each other's yearbook.

The Spaniard, Michael and I are the first to leave the campgrounds. The whole camp turns out at the parking lot to say good bye. It astounds us. Surprisingly, we are very nostalgic and teary. They keep waving until we are out of sight.

To recover from "Kampoo," a word used by the Koreans, and to do some touring, we travel north and west toward other little hill town villages in Honshu. Our plans later include visits to Kyoto, Nara, Takayama, and Tokyo before returning home. In many of the smaller towns there are no westerners in sight and almost no English spoken. This aspect of the journey is more difficult than anticipated. It is still very hot, communication continues to be exasperating, and making arrangements is not easy.

We encounter many surprises that reduce the strains of traveling in Japan. The small towns have festivals, and we are invited to join in one with the Obori dancing. I even win a door prize. We meet genuinely interested Japanese who make huge attempts to communicate with us. The everyday kindness and little courtesies ease the stresses as well. Everywhere we go there is excellent service. There is real pride is assisting others. It is a Japanese trait that we admire greatly.

Happy Birthday, Bonnie

To celebrate my birthday, we reserve an upscale Japanese Royokan (Inn). It costs us US$150 for a one-night stay including meals, cheap by Japanese standards. We are excited when we are picked up by the Japanese couple at the train station. They have a fancy van with a TV. They speak very little English.

Our inn is disappointedly located in a suburban area. But we don't complain. Huffing and puffing, we haul our elephants up the stairs. Once again, we can hardly fit the suitcases in the room. The expensive (for us) Royokan has a tiny room and a shared toilet. We smile at each other and try to be cheerful. To rid ourselves of travel fatigue, we take a nice hot Japanese bath downstairs. For dinner, we sample from an exquisite display of unrecognizable but wonderfully tasting food, sans birthday cake. We roam the area after dinner to locate a bar to have a celebration drink. No luck.

We return to our little cubbyhole of a room and plop down on our twin beds. Before long, the distinct sound of high pitched whistles engulf us. It gets louder and louder until we hold our ears. We soon discover that the local train runs right next to our window. How lucky can we get? We laugh until we are crying. We put in our earplugs, turn off the lights, and sleep in spite of the noise. A birthday I won't ever forget.

Knowing When to Go Home

There are daily joys and delights of discovering the many shrines, temples, and life in Japan. However, the heat, daily struggles with language, and the high cost of living is taking its toll. Our budget is suffering with the bad exchange rate. We are staying at pensions and hostels, and our average nightly rate is $100. Food is also a problem. We've had more rice and noodles than we can stand, and Michael is rapidly wasting away. Eating fruit, meat, or an occasional cup of coffee is practically out of our price range. A grapefruit is $5 and coffee $4 a cup. Lately, we buy our food at an equivalent of a "7-Eleven" and eat in the park.

It is often the little things, after a continuing series of episodes, which trigger a major decision. The final straw occurs when we investigate a night in an air-cooled movie theatre. The cost is $18 per ticket, so we don't go. Something clicks inside us. As we sit on the steps of a bank building, I say, "I think it is time to go home." Michael is astonished because I'm always the one that wants to continue trekking on.

We evaluate our situation. It is impossible to eat anything other than rice and noodles without paying a hefty price. Accommodations are expensive. The weather continues to be extremely hot and humid, which makes travel hard. We have seen many wonderful sites and have had more experiences than we ever could have dreamed of. We are becoming tired of traveling. At this point, the decision becomes easy. It is definitely time to return home to our native soil.

Sayonara, Japan.

Japan Notes

Japan is an extremely interesting culture. We have so many stories to share, but it is hard to incorporate all the many experiences into this chapter. We want to reinforce the fact that these are our impressions based on our experiences and may not be generally true. Here are a few more general impressions.

Japan's population is around 126 million and 75% of these live in urban areas. An island nation, Japan is ethnically and culturally homogeneous. Its government system is organized similar to the British Parliamentary system.

This is a very neat and clean country. Everyone picks up after themselves. There's no litter to be seen anywhere. There is a special garbage can for each type of item. The streets, sidewalks, and even gutters in the villages and small towns we visited are swept clean. The sense of order is extraordinary. Everyone knows to put things back the way they found it.

When you cross the street at a stoplight, you are treated to a melody. Advertising in the cities is overwhelming and old style hawking still exists. In the countryside, however, there is very little of this.

This is a wealthy country. It is also expensive. Vending machines are everywhere and have many things you want. As toilets go, some are hard to figure out. There are lots of buttons and knobs that squirt water. There are also the old style "squatters."

We take our shoes off everywhere and replace them with slippers that are provided. There are even special shoes for the bathroom. Bathing in Japan is a unique and wonderful daily experience. First, you sit on a little bench. You clean yourself using a water hose, bucket, scrub brush, and soap. After you are clean, you enter a steaming tub (that is often used communally in the lodging). You do not ever cleanse yourself in the tub. After drying, you then get into a clean yukata (robe) and return to your room.

Lessons Learned from the Work Camp

- The learning is in the doing. In this case, working physically hard to help others accomplish their goals helps with understanding more about Japanese culture and yourself.

- When you don't have command of a language you can find other ways of expressing yourself, including body movements, written language, and pictures. This all takes considerable energy and imagination.

- Language can be a barrier in communicating, but it is possible to make meaningful connections in other ways.

- Deprivation of comforts and familiar food generates thankfulness and gratefulness.

- Creative solutions (hokey pokey) are often the most simple ideas.

- Knowing when to stop and go home is important.

- A smile goes a long way.

- Working hard and taking orders from younger individuals teaches many lessons about our adaptability and team spirit.

Questionnaire

1. When was the last time you extended yourself physically?

2. Have you put yourself in situations that were uncomfortable? If so, what did you learn?

3. How adaptable are you in situations that require major lifestyle adjustments?

4. When was the last time you were expected to follow orders even when the orders didn't make sense? How did it make you feel? How did you respond?

Japan Travel Tips

Though ATM's were hard to find in Japan, it is safe to carry money bills.

The Internet cafes were not as abundant as we anticipated.

If you can't travel lightly, use the train lockers for daily, or several days, of storage. Be sure to check out the time limits. At one point we stored luggage and then discovered the time limit was only 24 hours. Another time, we were able to communicate with the train agent and got extended time on the locker.

"No Jet-Lag" is a homeopathic remedy for travel fatigue, www.nojetlag.com. Made in New Zealand

Chapter 10

Re-Entry Blues and Renewal

*What we call the beginning is often the end.
And to make an end is to make a beginning.
The end is where we start from.*
—T.S. Eliot, *Little Gidding*

Preparing for Transitions

How do you decide when it is time to come home? How do you notify your family, friends, and employer? What emotional preparations do you need to make in order to leave your time-off experience and reenter your old life?

Here is an excerpt from our diary of what not to do: After we make our precipitous decision to leave, we get on the phone immediately and arrange our flight to route through Seattle so we can visit with my daughter and family. The next morning, we take a train back to Kyoto, then on to Tokyo's Narita airport. Ten hours later we are in Seattle. In all, it takes us only twenty-four hours from the time we decide to leave Japan to when we get off the plane in the US. It isn't nearly enough time to adjust to the idea of returning home. There is no transition time.

In retrospect we would have done things differently. It takes some time just to acknowledge that you are leaving a special time in your life—there will be some sadness, good byes, and a mental adjustment. In most accounts that we have read about, the return into the old life is difficult. However, there are some ways to make the adjustment easier. One of our colleagues planned his reentry time table so that he would have several weeks in a quiet place in the US before going back to work and facing all the home and life responsibilities. As you will hear from our account, we eventually backtracked and did just that.

Plan for Your Arrival

If you know exactly the date you will return and you are out of the country, you might plan to locate yourself in a peaceful cottage or cabin to slowly make the cultural as well as mental adjustment. Make reentry part of your planning from the beginning and prior to announcing when you will return to work and home base.

If you aren't sure of your return date, or if you change your arrival date, be sure to notify friends and family in advance. In particular, make sure the changes don't affect your job. Several things happened to us because we didn't give anyone warning about our decision to return early.

For one thing, we had no opportunity to let our family know about our arrival. And so, there is no one to greet us when we arrive. In fact, my family in Seattle is gone for the weekend, and my sister is also unreachable. Needless to say, it is a very anticlimactic welcome home.

Culture Shock

If you have been living in another culture, expect to be surprised at things you once took for granted. Expect to feel dizzy, out of sync, like a stranger in your own country.

For us, the culture shock was immense. We booked ourselves into a little Hampton Inn near the airport. The cool temps in Seattle were most welcome after hot Japan. We are overwhelmed with the luxury of this hotel; a queen-size bed, a TV, microwave, refrigerator, and a huge bathroom. The swimming pool and workout room is amazing to us. It feels like the Ritz. The breakfast buffet is free and has more and richer food than we have seen in weeks. After this last year's experiences, we are overwhelmed and somewhat embarrassed by the quantity. We didn't see such food excess in many places around the world.

Reconnecting with Others

No matter how well you prepare yourself for the initial meetings with family, friends, and colleagues, communication will be awkward. After all, you have been away and many new things have happened to you—and to them. Be patient with yourself and others. Let things flow naturally. The sharing and old bonds will help you through eventually. Trust that you will find ways to meaningfully reconnect.

In our case, our family eventually emerges forty-eight hours after our arrival, and the welcome home is joyous. We feel like fish out of water. How do we connect again? How do we even begin to tell some of the stories? We have changed. They have changed.

My twelve-year old grandson now stands at six feet tall and is a little man. He is very interested in every aspect of the trip and has many questions especially on Japan, which he has studied. Showing our photos helps us explain our year away, and soon the stories begin to flow. Slowly, we begin to get reacquainted again

Michael is anxious to see his family, so he leaves after four days to connect with them. I decide to stay on longer to visit. Coincidentally, his welcome home is also disjointed. It turns out that family has plans for the weekend, and they aren't available.

Home Sweet Home?

If you decide to come back without any advance preparation, you may be in for some set backs. If you have a roommate, s(he) may not be expecting you. Or, if others have lived in your home, it may not be ready yet—as was the case with our home.

Worse yet, we discover that our home is not immediately livable—it is like Odysseus landing in Ithaca (chaos). Our family members have shielded us from some of the house disasters:

> Disaster 1: A broken water heater on New Year's Eve has damaged some of our stored household furniture.

> Disaster 2: Our tenant left unexpectedly in July, leaving behind a mess of broken appliances, badly stained rugs, and badly spotted walls.

Fortunately, Michael's son has looked after our house and was clever enough to arrange for financial compensation for damages. We are extremely grateful. At least we will have some money to fix the mess. After we get over the shock, we realize these are only inconveniences. The house is not seriously damaged, and what seemed disasters can be repaired. We realize how flexible we have become since traveling, and we don't let the little stuff bother us. We will survive this initial home reentry.

Putting Sabbatical Flexibility Lessons to Practice

We had no idea that we would immediately be tested in our new skills of being flexible. However, we were suddenly confronted with situations we hadn't counted on. For a week we stay with family and friends. Finally, we decide we need to be in our own home even without furniture.

We find ourselves living like we did in Japan, on the floor with a mattress. We can't find our silverware so we use our new Japanese chopsticks, which were gifts from one of our Japanese hosts. This whole situation begins to take on a humorous side and we have a huge chuckle. Little by little we put things together so we can live in the house. I visit my sister and get all the bills and papers back. Suddenly, we realize how nice it has been without that responsibility. We feel weighted down again.

Change and Adjustments

Even though there was news available along the way, many local things change. Expect the unexpected. You need to accept that a lot has happened while you were gone! Recognize why you are so uncomfortable, and use it help you understand. William Bridges, author of *Transitions*, says, "Recognize that transition has a characteristic shape—things end and things begin anew."

We are very disoriented. According to Bridges, "disorientation is meaningful but not enjoyable." So much of our former life has changed since we have been away. Our town has changed; restaurants have closed. There is a new multi-complex movie theatre in the neighborhood. Shops have come and gone. Catching up with local news and, of course, friends is a slow process.

We discover that we cannot take in too many things all at once. We purposely don't use our phones too much for several weeks. We call friends at a slow pace.

We advise you to pace yourself carefully instead of trying to get up to speed immediately. Give yourself at least a week to put your home in order before returning to work. If possible, alternate your schedule by working a few days in the office and work at home a few days. This will prevent information overload at work.

Working Again

When will you return to your job? How will you make the transition? We advise you to prepare a summary of all the lessons learned and how it will benefit your job. Don't forget all the nuances of the trip that promoted problem-solving, taking risks, communicating with others, and dealing with other cultures. If you have studied something during the time-off, be sure to show how it will benefit the company. Even if you don't feel it now, your trip has probably given you more confidence to handle new challenges. Brag a little. Let others know you are refreshed and have new ideas from your experiences.

You might even consider holding a lunch time discussion session for the company, showing some slides and talking about your experiences. This will also help you integrate the trip and ease the transition.

In our situation, Michael gets a call for work soon after our arrival home. Before he knows it, he is involved in putting together a proposal and making sales calls. He is overwhelmed but manages somehow. He knows that reintegrating with new technologies and catching up on a year's worth of happenings in the field will take considerable time and effort.

I start getting calls from the media and soon Fox TV wants me to do some interviews regarding the new census and its affects on work-family. I am surprised that my absence hasn't affected media interest. It is as though I never went away. It feels strange to put on my suit and dressy shoes. I feel as if I am having an out-of-body experience.

Retreating

After six weeks, we are still dizzy, confused, and unable to get ourselves together. This makes me feel like a weakling. I suggest to Michael that we need some quiet, adjustment time. He agrees. Our condo in Florida isn't being rented or used. We decide to take a break from the house chaos, proposal writing, and marketing and pull ourselves together.

After speaking to others who have gone on renewals, we are relieved to know we are not crazy. All the feelings of confusion are common after a long time away. One couple tells us they went to Hawaii for a few months to readjust. I'm suddenly feeling less guilty. After consulting the book *Transitions* I understand better why we are not yet adjusted.

We are in what is described as the "neutral zone"—disconnected from people and things from our past and emotionally unconnected to the present. We are experiencing the natural result of the ending process and getting ready for something new. The advice is to surrender and have some time to be alone—something we have already begun to do.

A friend explains his theory that the readjustment time takes equally long as the time away—a year to adjust? We are reminded that there is no one way to come home again after a year away. We are glad we can afford the extra time away from work. Time is needed to process. When you jump right in with many activities immediately, there is no time to figure things out.

Sorting Ourselves Out

We have taken action to readjust. It is warm and quiet in Florida. The condo is soothing; there is no household damage here. Once again, we are astonished by all the space and luxury surrounding us; sunken tub, air conditioning, swimming pool, tennis courts, etc. We take lots of time to walk, think, and write. Slowly, we begin to socialize with old acquaintances in Naples and tell our stories. Many people are puzzled that we put ourselves through so many uncomfortable situations. We realize the value of all our encounters, but it is hard to get others to see this. It is quite frustrating for us.

Making plans for the future is part of a reentry process. So we begin by sending out invitations to friends back home inviting them to four evenings of slide shows when we return. This feels right. It will accomplish many things. We will be able to tell our stories, process our trip, and have some fun. It will be a celebration of our return. These evenings were a huge success. Along with our slides, we included the food and music of our travels. I even perform flamenco. My debut!

Recognizing What We Have Learned

Take stock of what you have learned and acknowledge that your awareness and perceptions of the world have changed. Accepting and adapting to the "new you" will have its ups and downs.

For us, the culture shock is centered on the wealth in the US. Our new awareness contributes to negative feelings at the excess of material life. We have such a different view now. Many people take their heat, water, and air conditioning for granted. We are reminded of the cold nights in Seville and Jerusalem without any heat.

The US work ethic hits us hard after our travels. We are amazed by the work and business focus all around us. Workaholic has a new meaning. Time for socializing even with our friends and family is at a premium. They all make an effort to invite us for a welcoming dinner which is a real pleasure. It's the daily ongoing lack of time and spontaneity which bothers us.

Work Renewal Begins

After some down time, the payoff for our year away begins to take shape in our work life. There is new energy and ideas. If you take time-off, don't forget to tap into those new resources. You don't have to return to your job and do everything the same way. Allow yourself to see new ways of shaping the work you do to make a contribution for the organization. Do you see the organization in a different way? What suggestions can you make to improve it? Do you see better ways to problem solve based on your trip? What observations did you make during your time-off that can be applied to your job?

After a few weeks in Florida, I start to reap the benefits of the time away. I have incredible spurts of creativity, and before long I turn to marketing. First I send out press releases, which generate several articles. Next, I begin contacts with former clients, who are very intrigued with my stories. Soon, I realize that our renewal experience is an important story to share.

Michael and I discuss the possibility of conducting renewal/time-off workshops. Soon, we are very excited and develop a brochure. The ideas keep coming and I find myself enthused like I was fifteen years ago when I started my company. Giving our slide show for friends who are keenly interested reinforces our workshop ideas. Before we know it, we have assignments for early next year; a CEO forum, a community workshop, and a book contract.

Other opportunities present themselves through two former work associates. Since the time-off, I feel more open to exploring partnerships. These former colleagues provide a base for conducting training programs where I can use my old expertise and new creativity. In one instance, I'm able to work with a woman who has already established a workshop. Together we transform it and give it a boost from my new energy and new activities. It feels good to have this kind of energy and enthusiasm again.

The second example is a surprise. A woman who trains others in emotional intelligence is able to capture the essence of my time-off lessons and new passion. She sees the connection with her work and in creating new workshops on the topic of "renewal." Together we spend several months developing ideas, integrating her knowledge, and combining my knowledge and new found passion for work. The end result is several workshops that can be marketed through my company. The process and outcomes are exciting and invigorating. Likewise, Michael's work associates have some assignments for him when he returns home from Florida after a few weeks. We are delighted, as we need to bring in some income. For him, the renewal time has not affected working assignments.

Who Are We Now?

We are different but the same, a real contradiction. Time passes and we are able to get in a routine again. However, we have changed so much after the many varied experiences that we will never be exactly the same. Since traveling, our awareness of some excesses in the life around us has increased a lot. We observe many things about daily life in the US that we didn't notice as much before. In particular, we are amazed at how much waste and material excess there is in size of homes, automobiles, and even land use. As of this writing, California is going through an energy crisis. When we listen to all the comments and recommendations, we are reminded of how conscious and careful others are of energy usage in the countries we visited. Because of these experiences, we also have become very conscientious about the use of resources. It is frustrating for us to see the waste. We make an attempt to discuss this.

Conserving Resources, Living Simply

You may find that time-off will take you down new lifestyle pathways. Our renewal experiences have influenced us greatly. Now we begin to examine our lifestyle and integrate what we have learned from the permaculture experience in Australia, rationing water at the Dead Sea, conserving electricity in Spain and Israel, and the greening of Asia in Japan. How can we live a more simple life without abusing resources?

Our observations on car dependency and minimal walking in the US are somewhat annoying. We did so much walking during our year and it is more common in other countries not to depend so much on a car. When we first went to Florida on our return, we purposely did not rent a car. We tried to run errands by bike and on foot. However, because of the way newer cities like Naples are structured, we were only able to do this in a limited way. For the time being, we will continue to walk and bicycle and only use the car when it is truly necessary. For us, there is a mental sense of independence and freedom. We don't feel totally dependent and we feel good about being a model for others, especially our grandchildren. By using such resources as paper and water sparingly, we also represent a minority around us, but feel good about representing a larger worldview.

After not having a dryer for most of the year off, we are experimenting with ways to save resources by using a drying rack for towels and items that take longer periods to dry. I would like to hang my clothes out to dry in the summer but our shady yard isn't suited to this activity—nor would our neighbors approve.

All around us we often hear people complain about what they don't have. We are now sensitized as to how much we do have in this country and how much it is taken for granted. We are grateful in that knowledge and it makes our daily life more meaningful. We have learned to appreciate all that we do have and not to desire what others have or what advertisements say we should have. We continue to live simply and not buy unnecessary "stuff."

Health Care

After a year of postponing or ignoring basic health (we got teeth cleaning on the way), we encounter the outstanding health care, which we enjoy in this country and in our community. On our trip, we were surprised at how differently individuals look at health care. For example, in Spain we asked our friends to recommend a doctor with whom they confer regularly. When they get sick, they go to the clinic or hospital. In Israel, when I needed some pills for a stomach problem, I paid $100 for the consultation.

In Japan, the pharmacists act as health care consultants for uncomplicated situations and can prescribe certain medications. All in all, we did not find great fault with the systems. It just appears that the US has many more experts and facilities. The hospitals here are also very well equipped.

Renewal Flows

We are now part of the "real world" again, with the peaceful days of hiking and strolling at a minimum. Yet, there is calmness in our life that we didn't have previously. Our inner life has been nurtured over the year and it is easier to observe the daily chaos but not get entangled in it. We watch it, are aware of it, but can stand back from it. This continues to be the biggest challenge. We slip occasionally as we aren't perfect, but at least we are aware when this happens.

At times, there is a feeling of loneliness. We have turned ourselves upside down and many of our friends and family members are living the same lives. We don't judge this but know we don't quite fit in the way we used to. This is both good and bad news. We share in the best way we can and acknowledge that we have changed. We seek out new friendships that provide a way of connecting in meaningful ways. This is a positive outcome.

Keeping Renewal Friendships Alive

If you make new friends on a trip, staying connected is very rewarding. It keeps the memories up front even though you are back home. It takes time to correspond with the people we met and became friends with on the trip. Yet, the investment helps remind us the trip is still alive; it hasn't ended. We are lucky to have e-mail and the instant news of our friends abroad.

We have regular updates from our student friend in Seville. She has become more like an adopted daughter. Our initial connection with her was so meaningful that it has been easy to stay involved in her life. We enjoy her regular mail, humor, comments, and questions on US life.

We will have a rendezvous with Carmelita and Ray this coming summer when they visit their family in Canada. Our continuing correspondence has been helpful to

Carmelita's business. I feel very influential in helping her think through her marketing plans. I've also sent her some students from the US. Her warmth and passion for life comes through even in e-mail.

We have been deeply concerned about family and friends in Israel with the recent escalation in violence. It has been hard to hear about the random suicide bombings, and we worry about their safety. We are lucky that we were able to visit at a time that was somewhat safer.

Our Australian friends Bette and Bill have taken a renewal journey as well. We had an influence on their lives. We also got updates of a disastrous fire that almost destroyed their home and bushland garden. Fortunately, they were spared.

Our cousin in Switzerland had heart surgery but is recovering. Again, we are fortunate to have visited during a healthy time in his life. Timing is everything. We are glad we took the trip when we did. Much has changed since then; some good and some not so welcome.

Choices and The Overworked American

Coming to terms with the American lifestyle after being away is still hard for us and may be hard for you. One of the most poignant observations on returning home is the increase in long working hours and stress. When we left, it was a problem and, yet, it has increased even more. Job demands continue to escalate, as does the cost of living. It is a dilemma for everyone in the US. How do we fit in now with this all around us? What can we do to help reverse the effects of this lifestyle? How can we sensitize people to the critical, creative, and self-fulfillment need to better balance, time and money in this life?

The answers are not simple, but we feel stronger about saying "no" to things that add to the stress of life. In many ways, this simple concept is what I was teaching in my consulting work before leaving on the renewal. What is different now is that we have stepped away long enough to see other cultures having a more moderate work life and had time to reflect and see how our own energy has been replenished. It is easier for us to be clear and show others that there are always choices. Even in an economy that is unstable, it is possible to make choices for yourself and family that lead to a healthier lifestyle.

Our observations point out that it is the little things that make the difference in life's daily routines. If you listen to a morning news report that features killings and disasters throughout the world, and also read the newspapers that reinforce this, you begin the day with stress. Everyone is used to having the TV on regularly. As you recall in a previous chapter, we did not have TV or regular newspapers during our travels. Our habits changed during the course of the year and we have replaced old habits with more mindful activities.

The choices we make now are not to put the TV on in the morning and restrict reading newspapers to two or three times a week. We balance our reading and gathering of information with magazines and TV programs that promote a well-rounded understanding of the world and ourselves—as opposed to tabloid news. It is a choice and a habit as well. When the telephone rings, we don't always run to answer. We took the telephone out of our bedroom. We are still resisting the cell phone.

Napping became a regular part of daily routine this past year. It is hard to give it up and we value the results—more energy spread out throughout the day. Although we don't have the same siesta routine now, we take fifteen minutes in the afternoon to close our eyes and rest. When we are in a car or out and about, we have found creative ways to have a rest time in the car, on a park bench, on a blanket. I also consciously schedule appointments with clients so that the 2:00-3:00 time is open for a rest.

Because we value our lifestyle, which isn't filled with overwork, we still must be conscious of our budget. Therefore, the daily choices to eat out or buy things are carefully determined. We are constantly evaluating whether or not we need an item before we purchase it. We cook at home most of the time with a weekly night out. None of these choices make us feel in any way deprived. We are enjoying a more peaceful and balanced life by living within a modest budget.

Mindfulness and Reflective Practices

In previous chapters, we discussed the rewards of having the time to think, observe, and be more reflective. This has had a very positive aspect on our inner and outer lives. We want to continue in that direction. Daily, we integrate mindfulness and meditative practices to continue to heighten our awareness and manage the stress of daily living. We don't want to fall back into old patterns, which is so easy to do. Fortunately, we have each other to help reinforce positive practices. I highly recommend a class or group activity that can get you started in some of these practices. It is easier to make a change when you have a support system or person. Also, there are some recommended books at the end of this chapter that we continue to use in our daily practices.

Renewal is a Work in Progress

Every week a new idea or revelation pops up. We better understand how long ideas take to percolate and get actualized. We made a lifestyle change for one year and we are still reaping the benefits. Still, we continue to question how we will live out the rest of our lives. We ponder daily how to balance work, interests, volunteer time, family, friends, and travel within our budget. The difference now is that we truly believe there are many choices. In addition, we understand that making a change doesn't mean it is forever. A decision can be reversed. We have learned that there are so many ways to live a meaningful life, and we will continue to explore what is best for us at each stage of our life in the future.

The trip helped us to be less afraid of taking risks. The year away has given us strength, understanding, confidence and a healthy perspective on our lives. We are less likely to operate out of fear. We are more likely to continue to experiment with our lives. This gives us enormous choices in our work and life.

The serendipity we experienced and were able to take advantage of daily during our trip isn't the same now. However, it does exist in small ways. A recent weekend trip to Wisconsin opened a surprise door. We saw a poster advertising an evening lecture on archeology in a small town, Mt. Horab. As it turns out, the lecturer is a well-known anthropology expert from the Field Museum in Chicago. (He has a weekend home in Wisconsin.) One of his projects involves research in New Guinea. Since this is a place I have always wanted to explore, I immediately view this as a volunteer opportunity for the future. I discuss this with him after the lecture and follow up with an e-mail. Now, we are beginning a dialogue on the possibilities.

The year-off has taught us to act now when a situation presents itself and not to think on it too long. We continue to explore new paths. Our eyes are more open now and we are more alert to what might be another adventure.

One of our renewal goals was to be more authentic and true to ourselves. Clearly, this is a life-long endeavor. Yet, we are closer now than before the trip. It is the self-awareness and the choices we make every day that bring us closer to our authenticity. We have taken the first critical step by taking time out and reflecting and trying some new things.

The next challenge is to continue on that path of awareness, action, and self-checks. Are we living according to our values? Are we walking the talk?

As you recall, when I left for my renewal I was burned out. Now, I am definitely refreshed and replenished in many ways. My mind is less cluttered with negativity and the old stress is gone. I am feeling passionate about work and new lifestyle opportunities. I reaped more than I expected on this journey. I didn't expect to learn so much about myself, Michael, and the cultures of the countries we visited. In my estimation, the investment in time far surpassed any expectations on renewal.

Michael is continuing his self-exploration through a series of workshops. He also takes time to pursue his intellectual interests through classes and daily reading. He is also catching up on new technology by taking some Internet courses. Michael feels he learned how not to grow old gracefully. That is, he is stronger having taken on new challenges and having experienced physical and mental discomfort. Thus time-off has provided some direction for the future. Take more chances, be more open to "yes."

Renewal has also meant greater appreciation for the things and people around us. The comforts of home, our friends, family, community, work, and work associates have taken a new significance. The time-off has provided better perspective on these. Renewal has provided more current focus on what's important, in addition to the realization that this is subject to further changes.

What's Next On The Horizon?

When you return home, you can give yourself permission to lift the veil of limitations on your life. If nothing else, the renewal year taught us this. As we consider our health and age (58 and 62 years), we know that time is ticking away for us. As of now, our health is good. However, we will continue to take advantage of life's joys before we fall apart.

I continue to live out my passion for flamenco dance by taking a weekly class and doing an occasional demonstration for others. Michael is more involved in teaching grandchildren the values of simple living and about nature. We are both more active in promoting conservation.

We daydream about the next trip. It will probably be a shorter one—possibly a month in Chile. We plan to look for a volunteer experience again. Volunteering allow us to travel more frequently within a budget.

We both miss the nature trails, and it is a struggle to live in the Chicago area where there is more concrete than open space. Do we move? If so, where? We have family, friends, work connections and many roots here. What opportunities will we lose if we move? Neither Michael nor I are ready to retire. What can we do if we moved away from Chicago? These are questions we are asking now.

I have been exploring ideas that will simplify our lives and untie us from owning a home in Evanston. Maybe we could rent and travel around the country—a few months in our condo in Naples, a few months in Seattle near family, and a few months visiting other friends? Maybe another trip to Australia to see how the Bushland Educational Center is doing? These are the ideas we are playing with now.

It is still too soon to make a definite plan. We agreed to give ourselves one full year before making any other changes. When the year is up, we will reevaluate our situation again.

Reflections on Traveling as a Couple

In preparing for our trip, we never fully considered what it would be like to be together twenty-four hours a day for a year. Even though we did some separate activities along the way and had a month's separation, we were together most of the time and grew immensely strong as a couple. The fact that we shared so many adventures together is a binding factor in our relationship. When we reminisce, one of us always remembers something that the other doesn't. It keeps us laughing and smiling. We keep our adventure alive just by being together.

We also developed skills on how to compromise. There was no way we could have survived without a lot of give and take. Learning to be acutely aware of each other's moods and needs are skills that improved over time and continue to enrich our relationship today. There is also a lot of mutual respect for each other and the challenges we encountered and solved together. In the future, if I ever get lost or have a problem to solve, it is Michael that I want by my side.

Integrating What We Learned While Away

> *Seeking the truth about ourselves also includes a willingness to allow ourselves to be changed. Only by releasing the old ways, and enduring the loss of former behaviors and attitudes, can we then make the way for new ways.*
> —Paula Haynes, *What Are You Doing With the Rest of Your Life? Choices in Midlife*

After our trip, Michael and I discovered we had changed in many unexpected ways. Renewal embraces change and growth. Acknowledge that this is part of the process, should you choose to take time-off. Seek the truth, and that will allow you to be changed. You may find that you need fewer possessions. For example, we are amazed at our reaction when uncovering clothes and accessories that have been stored away for a year. We haven't missed them and feel we don't need them! For us, this process continues by giving and throwing many things away regularly. Or, you may find value in living a simpler lifestyle. We acknowledge the need for technology but don't feel impelled to buy all the new gadgets. As of this writing, we still don't have a cell phone or cable TV. There is value in limiting daily newspapers.

Your need for connecting with nature may increase. We found on returning that going to movies, plays, and concerts again has its joys. But it doesn't replace the many trails we hiked and the pleasure we got from our outdoors time. You may use the things you learn on your trip and adapt them to your lifestyle when returning home. For example, we became so aware of the advantages of using native vegetation that we suggested a butterfly garden using native vegetation to our condo association in Florida.

Volunteering may become contagious. We enjoyed volunteering immensely in other countries. When we returned, we joined Habitat for Humanity to build houses for those less privileged.

You may find yourself more upbeat and less affected by daily ups and downs. We are more flexible now and don't take things so seriously. Prior to our renewal, some situations that seemed more difficult to deal with are no longer a big deal.

Consider, too, that you may enjoy cross cultural exchanges so much that you will want to continue seeking them out in some way. We were treated so well in other countries. We are more willing to open our home to others and to make new friends. We go out of our way to invite new friendships into our lives. We also want to join Servas or other organizations that promote cross-cultural experiences and home stays. As a result of your experiences, you may even find your habits regarding time have changed. We are conscious about allowing more time for others. We are leading busy work lives again, but there is a good balance.

You may become open to many varied experiences and less sensitive to situations that present some discomfort.

When nothing seems impossible, exploration is fun—there are fewer restrictions for where you sleep and what you eat. You can acknowledge that there is far less to fear about the unknown when nothing bad happens for a year. All the warnings and fears of the world outside the US were dispelled on this trip. You can see yourself now a little like a gypsy. The comforts of home, the need for the best coffee and foodstuffs don't necessarily make us happy. Living without hot water, heat, and a comfortable bed is liberating. Even your communication style may change. For instance, we gained a new awareness about how to communicate. We know we can make ourselves understood even with limited language skills.

Old fashioned hard work can be fun. We notice that we are more open to untraditional activities and are reminded about the value of a day's hard physical work. We are not too proud to do menial jobs—cooking, cleaning ironing, weeding etc., in exchange for a bed and food. It is humbling, and we have attained new physical strengths which were formerly underdeveloped and unappreciated by us.

You may now be amazed at the power of doing nothing. We can endure long periods of unplanned time and appreciate the value of it. Finding a good companion to live and travel with is a bonus as we found out. This is good news for retirement.

Another valuable discovery is that being connected doesn't require a telephone, newspaper, or TV. You may be more aware and appreciative of the wonders of the world—people doing interesting and innovative things—and much of it not for money or fame. This is a value to treasure and incorporate into our lives. There are courageous people living difficult lives without complaints. They are an inspiration!

Not surprisingly, your attitude about work may change. Work is not so important as we think, but connecting with others is one of the most important aspects of human growth.

Taking time to climb hills and mountains can be a heavenly experience, and they are the things you will want find time for in your life.

Family is important worldwide and extremely important to us. Be aware of it and nurture those relationships often. The US is a most innovative country—and a place where women have far better opportunities and more freedom of choice. We are materially rich, but have lost a lot of community spirit and joy in the simple things. Being accepted for who you are and not what you do is extremely rewarding.

Ultimately, cultural differences can be bridged with a willingness to understand and not judge others. A smile and the willingness to listen goes a long way. You can find kindness, trust, and helpfulness outside of your familiar world. The physical beauty of the planet is never to be taken for granted. It must be treasured and cared for.

We will never be the same people after this trip, and it will be difficult to integrate all that was learned and appreciated. The next chapter of our lives will be the challenge of reevaluating where we want to live and what we want to do with the rest of our lives. The best is yet to come.

Lessons Learned

- Build in adjustment time when you return home.

- Allow transition time before you leave your time-off experience.

- Do some research before you have someone live in your home. (I would do it again, but not rush the process.)

- Find a variety of ways to share your time-off stories with others. It helps to process.

Chapter 11

Making Your Decision

Daring to realistically assess where we are in the life span takes courage. Before we gain this courage, we must pass through the ordeal of acknowledging our fears about the future. Fear makes us feel helpless and can be a barrier to choosing well.
—Paula Haynes, *What Are You Doing With the Rest of Your Life?*

Now that you have journeyed along on our renewal, perhaps you have already thought about taking your own time-off journey. Maybe you've explored what you would like to learn, where you would like to go, and whether or not you want to try volunteering. By now, you probably have a good idea of the emotions and transitions involved in taking a renewal journey. You have also gained knowledge of many travel 'do's and don'ts.' And so, you may be convinced that you can't wait another day to embark on this next stage of your life! However, don't buy that renewal ticket just yet. To make your renewal a success, you need to plan. And while there is a lot to consider, this process can be fun and exciting, too.

I'm sure you have fears about taking risks in your life. You're not alone. We had much trepidation before determining what was the best way to plan time-off and still meet our financial needs and not sabotage our careers. There were many lengthy discussions hashing out the gains and possible losses. I'm a natural risk taker. I have an unwavering belief that there is little to lose and nothing is inscribed in stone.

When I first approached Michael with the idea of taking time-off, he was only mildly interested. Michael had been working as an independent logistics consultant for five years. Formerly, he spent twenty years working for the Quaker Oats Company. He has been generally happy with his assignments. His children and grandchildren live nearby.

If you have a partner who does not share your risk-taking approach, then your job is to listen, understand, be patient, and then deal with the concerns one by one. Can you identify with any of his or her fears? Have compassion when these fears arise. Remember that unplugging, even for a temporary period of time, usually raises a lot of important issues and legitimate concerns.

What are some of the fears and doubts either you or a partner may encounter? Some of the major ones are as follows: How can I leave a profession (income) and homey conveniences for a length of time without losing control of finances? Will I be able to reenter and continue my work, or am I permanently cutting myself off? Could I trust the renting our house/apartment and having people oversee finances? Who will take care of maintenance and the perceived risks of roofs leaking, burglary, and who knows what else? How will my elders, children and grandchildren react? Who will care for our pets? Am I too old for this kind of a trip? What if we get sick in a foreign country? How can I make a lengthy trip if I have a chronic health condition?

Here is a questionnaire to help you get started with your own assessment. It's important that you be honest with your feelings when answering. Only then can you face your fears and take the steps necessary towards renewal.

If you find that you are failing in the risk and trust areas, you might want to discuss this with a personal friend or colleague. Ask yourself if this is affecting your work-life goals. What are the consequences if you choose to take no risks in your life? Is fear or anxiety preventing you from being the best in all areas of your life? This exercise may help you to learn more about yourself and allow you to make some small changes. When in doubt, get some counseling.

Risk and Trust Questionnaire

1. What is your greatest fear regarding taking time-off?

2. Do you know anyone who took time-off?

3. When was the last time you took a risk? What was the outcome?

4. Do you believe that your success depends on face time at work?

5. Do you believe you could find another job if you have to?

6. Can you remember a time when you just day-dreamed? Describe how it felt?

7. Do you have faith in your decisions about what you need?

8. Do you worry about spending your retirement savings?

9. Are you afraid to travel alone?

10. Do you have difficulty imagining a new way of living your life, even temporarily?

Negotiating for Renewal Time

If you want to hit the pause button for an extended period of time, you may need the help and support of others in your life to make it happen. This means you will have to negotiate and sell your ideas to others. With whom will you need to negotiate? It may be a supervisor, co-worker, trusted relative, business partner, a life companion, or other support people that can determine the success of your adventure.

In my case, it was my partner/husband who was the one I had to sell on the idea of taking a renewal. Because I am the owner of a business, I could work out my time-off with clients. Michael, however, was coming from a very different point of view. To convince him of the benefits, I used negotiation techniques.

When you think about it, life is all about making deals—I get something, you get something. You may find it useful to make a list of the pros and cons, pluses and minuses, and costs and benefits. I'm sure you have been making deals in your life. For me, the possible losses were my sanity and professionalism. The gains were potential renewal and putting passion back into my everyday life.

First, you need to know the person or persons you are negotiating with. Awareness is key to good negotiations. I know, for example, that Michael is practical and logical. He questions and analyzes everything. Convincing him to take a year off was not going to be easy. My challenge was to sell him on the idea by clearly stating my case.

I thought carefully about Michael's "hot buttons"—things that interest him and the benefits of taking a year off. I reminded him of his favorite quote, "The unexamined life is not worth living." I reflected on his past history of leaving the corporate fold for independent work and having done considerable international work in Europe, Latin America, Mexico, and Singapore. He is most aware of dislocation, adventure, excitement, and learning in new cultures, so this is not a new concept to him. He knew the good, the bad, and the ugly.

He loves exploring cultures, hiking, digging into new ideas and feeling productive. He even investigated the idea of joining the Peace Corps a few years earlier and also dreamed of going to Japan to work. His idea of time-off was work related or possibly volunteering abroad. I was only slightly interested in working, but I agreed to consider it. So, I continued to think about presenting all possible benefits for taking time-off. These included: learning a new language, uncovering work possibilities, searching for a new career, gaining knowledge, climbing mountains, and wandering, which he loved as a child.

Whether you are going on a traditional academic or corporate sabbatical or not, it is good to evaluate what you know about the people with whom you negotiate daily. How aware are you of their interests and history? This knowledge might save you time when you need to take time-off for personal reasons. It might save you hassles with your boss, elder, or friend, or even teenager.

Ideas and Self-assessments

Use the following assessments to help improve your negotiating skills and turn your dreams into a reality.

Making a deal

As discussed earlier, you aren't alone in this decision. No matter with whom you have to negotiate, you must be creative and have a well thought out plan.

If you are employed by an organization

Do your homework. Investigate your company's policies regarding time-off. Start with human resources, but use the grapevine as well. If the company doesn't have a formal policy, someone probably has negotiated a sabbatical informally somewhere in the organization. Enlightened managers often allow time-off on a case by case situation. Even if there is a policy, many managers won't buy into the idea unless you have an excellent plan. (See a list of companies and resources at end of this book.)

If you have your own business or are a consultant

Even if you run your own business, you will want to have work when you return. If you have had a good relationship with your customers and clients, communicating your objectives is essential and shouldn't be a problem. In many cases, customers and clients can feel abandoned when you leave. Having a temporary replacement is a good way to instill confidence.

Give enough notice to current clients. Be sure to allow enough time to finish active projects so you don't leave anyone in the lurch. Inform clients that you will be available by e-mail for any issues that may arise when you are away. In my case, I started notifying clients nine months in advance and continued to outline the benefits of my time-off. As a work-life consultant, I felt very strongly about "practicing what I preach." For me, it was a natural extension of my current consulting. In many ways, I became a role model in my profession. Michael was working in partnership with another consulting firm. He also timed leaving to coincide with projects that were winding down. He kept up good communication with the consulting firm while away, and when he returned work opportunities were waiting.

Have a clear objective and communicate it

If necessary, say it in corporate-speak. You now know what time-off means to you. Now it is your challenge to turn that objective into something the decision-makers will understand. Communication, choice of words, and attitude are crucial here. For example, consider using a different word than sabbatical. Some managers won't get it. Try some words like extended leave, renewal time, time to broaden my horizons, or time-off to learn.

For example, if you are planning extended time-off from work, you won't want to start with negatives such as "I'm really burned out by this job." Instead, try to start with a positive statement such as, "I know how much productivity means to you. I have found something that will get me going and help make this department the best in the company. Are you interested?"

Timing is everything. You'll want to hold your discussion at a time when the manager can really listen and isn't distracted. Take him/her to lunch. Be upbeat and enthusiastic—as if you have made a great discovery. Keep the energy going even if you notice the news isn't being received well.

Use active listening techniques such as "I understand how you must feel." or "You might feel I am abandoning the ship. Well, I'm actually going to increase your revenue in the long run by taking this time-off."

What's the Game Plan?

Here are some important questions to consider to make sure you are well prepared. Who will replace you? How will you train someone? How will you tell co-workers? Will you communicate to the office or do you want to be free of all work responsibilities? Will you come back? Is this a paid sabbatical or partial pay? Are benefits included? Are benefits possible without pay? Are you willing to come to work an extra day for a month to save up a bank of time? Can you use your sick time and vacation time to add towards extended time-off?

Sell It with All Your Creativity

Go for it! You won't get what you want unless you can get your ideas across with clarity and strength of purpose. Here is where those selling skills kick in. If you have been creative with your plan, you will have a list of the benefits for your intended trip—that study program, new skill development, bike trip, cooking school, or archeological dig.

If your time-off is somewhat related to your job, it's probably not going to be a problem. For example, if the company has a social service program, connections with an academic institution, industry association, or sees value in a study program related to current or future work, then you may strike a deal. But, let's face it, most of us want to do something "out of the box"—at least once. So if you decide to do something unrelated to your job, how can you justify it?

For example, if I had to justify taking flamenco classes in Spain I would have promoted the study of family life and work life in Seville and learning Spanish. Believe it or not, sitting in cafes helped me to understand the work ethic of Spain. I could have easily written a paper on the differences between American work and family life and the Spanish. Another benefit of choosing to study the Spanish language in today's global society was that of adding skills to my repertoire.

Bring on Those Objections

Get armored and ready! Will you be prepared for objections? If you do your homework, you will have an answer for every objection. Statistics, examples, and stories will help you win your case. Check Working Mother's Magazine and their list of "100 Best Companies." They will inform you of companies offering sabbaticals. In addition, The Society of Human Resources will have some up to date statistics on sabbaticals. Use the Internet to help with your search. Believe it or not, layoffs in the US have promoted more corporate sabbaticals, as well. It sounds like a contradiction, but many employers would prefer that employees take a sabbatical instead of losing them to another employer.

To ensure success, practice your presentation with a tape recorder and in front of a mirror. Give the presentation to your most objective friends who can critique and help you deal with anticipated objections. Your ability to come back with a positive response and with absolute confidence is the most important skill.

> You may need more than one conversation to sell your idea. For most busy managers, the initial shock may be so great that he or she can't give you a simple answer on the first go around. How badly do you want this? Be clear on what you are willing to compromise and live with. If you can't get all the time you need, what will work for you?

Belief: It's Your Strongest Asset

Don't be discouraged. If you believe in the need for your time-off, you'll find the inner and outer resources to sell your idea. I would seriously consider some meditative time to help you gather the inner strength you will need. This will be your source of power. The powers of meditation and visualization will help you overcome your fears and keep you focused.

For example, when you reach a tentative decision about your time-off destination and objectives, sit quietly in a room or a park and begin to focus on your intent. Allow yourself to feel the textures of your planned idea. What sensorial feelings arise when your focus on it? Does it feel warm, peaceful, or does it have a light of energy and joy? Take deep breaths and focus on the positive energy your thoughts generate. When you go to your work space, keep those sensorial feelings with you. When you speak about your renewal intentions to others, recapture the joy and positive aspects from your meditative experience and use them to help others understand. The more you do this, the stronger you will feel about your decisions, and the easier it will be to help others visualize your intent.

When we were in our planning stages, I would routinely spend an hour each day to walk and meditate on the plan. I discovered that my fears about leaving my consulting practice would dissipate. Soon, the fears were replaced by excitement and a belief that it was okay to let go. Every time I felt frightened I would recreate the meditative experience to give me strength.

Persistence, Persistence, Persistence

Persistence often wins out if you state your case consistently and relentlessly. I persevered to convince Michael by focusing on the benefits and handling his objections. How long will this take? In our case, we kept the conversation going for over a month before an initial agreement was made. The conversation encompassed all the fear and trepidation related to taking time-off.

You have heard about the fears. Now, here are some of the benefits I stated over and over in various ways:

- "If we don't do this, we'll be stagnant."

- "We will regret not taking this opportunity while in good health."

- "What have we really got to lose?"

- "What endless possibilities and opportunities will present themselves to us?"

- "We can always find ways to make money."

- "We have faith in ourselves and will let things unfold as they are destined."

Another strategy is to recall what benefits and arguments you have used in the past that have been successful in selling an idea or achieving a goal. There are also external situations or factors in your life that will affect the decisions as well. For example, we received quite a bit of support from our friends and some support from our children. Our parents were deceased. Our last child was just getting married. (Don't let family stop you. In fact, many people have taken renewal time with family.) We knew our health was good, and we realized that if we planned creatively, we could probably fund the trip without dipping into our retirement funds.

Once we were in agreement we returned to our motto, "The unexamined life is not worth living," and set a date for beginning our journey—October, 1999. When you reach an agreement, relish and celebrate this special moment as the first of many. With decisions made, the excitement of exploring options begins!

Choosing a Traveling Partner

Sharing a trip with someone can make it more meaningful and less stressful, if it is the right person. It is a lot easier to problem solve and get around when there are two individuals sharing the responsibilities. However, if the goals aren't the same and compromise isn't possible, it could be a nightmare. Even under the best circumstances, there will be disagreements. The ability to compromise is a big issue. Michael and I had disagreements that required enormous problem solving and compromising to work things out.

If you aren't planning to travel with a spouse/partner, you may consider a friend for a traveling companion. Think carefully before you initiate the idea. It may be helpful to ask yourself the following questions: How well do you know this person? How flexible is he/she? How does this person handle problem solving situations? What traits irritate you, and could you live with them? What travel experience does that person have? What do you have in common? Can the individual compromise? How will you benefit from this particular trip partner?

Sharing responsibilities is also a big part of choosing traveling partner. In the beginning, Michael took much more responsibility because he was more fluent in Spanish. As time went on, I became more comfortable with language and could do more in terms of shopping, arranging for tickets, and calling for information. I made a conscious effort when we got to Australia to take on more responsibility for making phone call inquiries or arrangements. This is all part of the give and take on a trip of this length.

Before making a decision, you might consider a trial run—a short trip in your own locale. Learn about the person's habits and decision making process. Can you live with them? Travel is always stressful, especially when you are in a foreign country or gone for a long period of time. You will have to depend on this person for many things. You can avoid mishaps by being realistic about your needs and the other person's capabilities.

> *Making the changes necessary to improve the quality of your life requires a fierce commitment to continuous learning. And learning, whether about yourself, about others, about the ways of the world, or about the immensity of the mysterious universe, requires considerable courage.*
> —Joel and Michelle Levey, Living in Balance

Exploring Options

When was the last time you gave yourself permission to think about all the places you dreamed of visiting or all the things you would love to do and learn? When you consider the possibilities for travel and renewal, the list is endless—a trip down the Amazon, a retreat in Bali, volunteering in India, learning a craft, working on a dude ranch, or walking the Appalachian trail. You could go to one place for a year or break it up into a different place each month. We have traveled in the past and found that staying in one place for an extended time offers more cultural depth. If you have a year available, it is possible to do that. If you travel to more destinations, you have the chance to see more of the world. There are advantages to both approaches. It is merely a question of objectives and desires.

You could have a set plan to study or visit in one country and have some specific timetables and destinations that are preplanned. For those who like regularity and no surprises, it might be to your advantage to have a more set plan with flights, lodging, and activities determined in advance.

For individuals who like spontaneity, you may choose to wing it and make decisions along the way. Or, you may decide to combine both options—a little security and some surprises. However, at some point you listen to your heart and you begin to clearly see what you need. Also, when you are a couple, the trip has to accommodate the needs of both. By following the 12-Month Time-Line Chart that begins here and continues in Chapter 12, you'll be able to develop your plan more clearly.

Minus 12 Months—Decision Point

At minus 12 months your decision to take a renewal is a "go." Then the countdown continues for determining your options and coming to your decisions.

Minus 11 Months—Consider Options

Look into what you know from the past—other friends, associates. Learn from them. We were lucky to have close friends who taught English in Japan for two years. Their time-off experience was very positive. We spent several evenings looking at photos, probing, and learning about their experience. We left feeling very excited. Another couple took a year to explore their roots, study, and visit places they longed to see. Who do you know who has taken time out? What can you learn from them?

Minus 10 months—Making Choices

Eliminate options that don't seem appropriate for your goals. For example, after a month of going through the interview process to teach English in Japan, it became clear to us that such a program—with too much work and no flexibility—wouldn't allow us the type of a renewal time we desired. (We would have had to take two apartments. And, we couldn't be guaranteed a teaching schedule that was the same for both of us. Most importantly, the hours were long and rigid.) A rule of thumb—don't jump into anything your heart isn't into. It won't work in the long run, and you will have regrets. Be honest with yourself.

Dreams, Wish Lists, and Realities

Don't be surprised, worried, or disappointed if you need to go back to the drawing board. If you're like us, you'll discover that planning renewal time isn't as easy as it seems! Our experience tells us that it requires many in-depth discussions to make the year special. Just like other important decisions, it requires work. Here are some questions which might be asked at this stage of planning:

- "What will renew my spirit and my mind?"

- "How do I want to live the rest of my life?"

- "What chance things will point to new ways of living?"

- "What do I want to learn?"

- "What culture attracts me?"

- "What activity have I always wanted to undertake?"

- "What challenges do I want to encounter?"

- "What weather conditions are important to consider?"

What questions come to mind as you read the above list? One of your goals is to rethink the life you are currently living—that includes the work you are doing and the physical location of your permanent home. For example, my age and stage in life (late 50's) weighs on me. I want to be clearer about how my partner and I live out the rest of our lives. I want to be more authentic and clarify my "callings." What does your age and stage determine for you—more study, more exploration, more ease?

In the process, let your mind wander and begin to create a wish list. Let your imagination go as Michael and I did. Michael's wish list included doing something useful and challenging—possibly volunteering. His ideas included activities on how to be useful and productive. My wish list was more specific. Once I started the intellectual exercise, visions of beautiful Spanish skirts, colorful shawls, and glittering castanets swirled around me! At the top of my list was Spain—studying flamenco dance, and savoring the gypsy and cafe life. My recent experience studying flamenco dance began to influence my decisions. I came to the conclusion that one of my dreams was to study it further in Spain. The time was now to shed the corporate suits and trade them in for Spanish attire. I could feel the passion swelling up inside me. Yes, this is one of my renewal dreams.

Michael also turned to his dreams and desires. Israel was deep in his heart. He was born there, and we had never traveled there as a couple. Tears appeared in his eyes as he talked about his homeland and reconnecting with his childhood spirit. Going home sounded good to him. Feeling useful and gaining knowledge of the past were also important aspects, so he suggested that we volunteer on an archeological dig.

Working with the Aborigine community was also a dream of mine. Australia is a place I have visited seven times and which has held a strong attraction and spiritual resonance for me. We discussed my desire to return to Australia for one final walkabout—so it was agreed to go down under. Finally, we both held a desire to explore Japan, especially after all the research we had done up to this point. So, Japan became our final destination. The details of what, where, and how— would be left for another day. We wanted to embrace the excitement and joy of our decisions and trust that all the blanks in between would be filled in later. We toasted to adventure, renewal, and the unexplored life!

As you can see this process worked very well for us. If you are traveling alone, you can invite friends to brainstorm with you, as Michael and I did. This process of opening possibilities is more effective when you have some input. Take your time.

Fantasize and Daydream Exercise

What kind of a renewal time will work for you? Not everyone can take a year off, so what is possible for you to consider? One month, three months, six months, a year, or possibly two years?

Because it takes time to unwind from daily life and work habits, we advise you not to take anything less than one month. If you remember back to when you took your last vacation, it probably wasn't until the second week that you began to shed your worries, thoughts, and work-life responsibilities. In addition, it is very important that not all of your time is planned.

Now it's your turn to daydream and rid yourself of fears that may prevent you from a unique experience. Lie on your back or sit in a comfortable chair with your eyes closed in a quiet place. For about twenty minutes, imagine yourself doing something that brings joy to your heart. Visualize yourself in different settings. If nothing comes to your mind, try the exercise another day. Pick a time when you are not so tired—possibly on a weekend.

Another good way to help you decide is to ask the question: What would I do if I only had a year to live? You can also ask what regrets you have— what things have you always wanted to do but didn't take the time for? Don't wait until retirement. Do it now!

If you are still undecided, use some travel books to inspire you or talk with someone who has taken meaningful time-off. Invite some of your best friends to brainstorm with you. If this is a family exercise, let everyone have a chance to give an idea. Don't rule out those first ideas—they are probably the things you need the most. In fact, don't rule out any idea until you are absolutely sure it won't work.

If you find it difficult to let go and embrace a time-off direction, you may want to explore some of your deepest held values. Whether we want to admit it or not, values that we have grown up with affect our life's decisions. As you evaluate your circumstances, think about how your family values influence your decision making process. Do any of the following family values ring a bell for you?:

1. Being productive all the time is the best way to live your life.

2. Doing nothing is shameful.

3. Renewals are only for rich people or academics.

4. Taking time-off is selfish.

These are typical values that are often passed on from generation to generation. If my mother had been alive when we announced our renewal time, she would have been taken aback. Her depression era values included a strong, non-stop work ethic. In addition, she would have seen it as selfish to devote a year to one's passions. Unconscious obstacles from parental values often influence our decisions and make it hard to take the plunge. My advice is to be aware of them, but not let them deter your inner need for renewal or change.

Paula Payne Hardin, in her book *What Are You Doing with the Rest of Your Life?*, sums it up well:

> *Changing the old parental attitudes that have become life scripts for us requires hard work, courage, and persistence. Often the new approach will*

feel wrong, even selfish. Others may not like the changes and may try to make us feel guilty. The old behaviors feel "right" in some way, so moving from what seems familiar and secure to what feels selfish and strange can bring anxiety. But be assured that such anxiety is really a sign of progress. Often you will find unexpected reinforcement for your changes from unexpected sources.

What's Your Renewal Type?

What is it that you really need for renewal? What will put back some of that creativity and joy into your life again? There are many unique ways in which individuals can take negotiated time-off for renewal. For example, in 1976 I had an opportunity to go to Israel for one month. At that time, I was employed full time as a Montessori teacher. I had to sell my co-workers, as well as the administrator, on the idea of leaving the classroom for a month.

My negotiations included the goal of visiting Israeli schools and kibbutzim and bringing back information for the Montessori school. I pointed out that I would also accumulate educational materials with which I could build a curriculum. These were all good selling points. After I gave the school names of individuals who could replace me in the interim, permission to take leave was granted.

What follows are several examples of how you can choose to restart and renew your life. Each one has its own unique goals and timetable. See if any of them resonate with you.

Spiritual Renewal

- Alex and Sarah are workshop leaders and writers. Over the years, they studied various meditative practices. They felt strongly about making a long-term commitment to the art of meditation. They wanted to have a deeper understanding about themselves as well so they closed up their house and moved into a little temporary camp near the base of Mt. St. Helens.

Alex and Sarah joined a small community of other individuals also intent on enriching their inner lives. Their renewal time had a very different meaning to them. They meditated in silence for one year and in separate bungalows. Their courage to leave their business, friends, and family was far greater than any other story I have read about. As you can imagine, they emerged emotionally and spiritually very strong. The rewards for them continue to be uncovered. Their extraordinary work is helping others to maintain a balance through their writing and workshops. They continue to publish and help others to live a life of wholeness.

New Skills and Personal Fulfillment Renewal

- Paul is a professor and works in a medical center in Europe. He has taken a number of sabbaticals. Being an individual who believes in continuous improvement, he looked for an opportunity to in computer learning systems in Canada. He was offered a three-month project near where his children and grandchildren were living. It was an ideal opportunity for him to explore something new. He not only got renewed and energized through the new work experiences, but he was able to experience a different environment while enjoying the benefit of being close to his family.

Corporate Reorganizing as an Opportunity Renewal

- Bette Jackson—a human resource specialist—had an opportunity to take leave of her job during a reorganization. This included some severance pay. Instead of jumping into another job immediately, she decided to spend more time with her son. As a single parent, this was a meaningful opportunity. During the first two months, she focused on improving her physical health, redecorating, reading, and volunteering at her son's school. These were things that were difficult to do during her previous career.

One of Bette's passions is writing so she is taking time to write as well. This is another way to view time-off—by taking advantage of opportunities when mergers, reorganizations, and downsizing do occur. Ms. Jackson is getting revitalized and positioning herself for the next career move. She is operating from a position of strength—good physical and mental health.

A Mini-Renewal

- One example of a mini-renewal comes from Leslie, an international traveler, writer, and editor who convinced her partners in a small communications company to offer twelve days of time-off a year for each partner. This was done with very careful planning around client needs and down times on their projects.

From the USF study, (www.usfca.edu/fac-staff/bell/article21.html) "High achieving employees usually can't be given slow-go work assignments in an effort to let them rest up and refresh their energies. Such assignments would be seen by these employees and their peers not as a perk for performance but as a demotion of sorts, even if their pay did not change. Sun Microsystems, IBM, Cisco Systems and other computer companies have led the way in offering short-term renewals, or sabbaticals, to employees who have given their all to the job and are understandably near the breaking point. These mini-renewals typically last two to six weeks."

Traditional Academic Renewal with Family

- Joan works as an instructor at a community college. Feeling restless for more intellectual challenges, she took a six month leave to do a research project in Europe studying composition. She got eighty percent of her pay. Her family (husband and two boys) accompanied her. They spent three months in each country—France, Italy and Greece.

Joan's challenge was to help fill in the days for her family and still accomplish her academic goals. Her husband did some painting and they home-schooled their children. Joan emerged from the experience both intellectually invigorated and personally confident. "I can go anywhere and land on my feet." Upon her return she was able to immediately apply her research and integrate it into her work—an important professional goal for her.

Mark Shainblum, author of *And on the Seventh Year*... writes that "Professors often use sabbaticals to free themselves from day-to-day grind—The sabbatical must consist of a structured project with concrete, achievable goals" Academic sabbaticals encourage educators to immerse in a field, recharge and often rethink teaching. It also offers talented researchers an opportunity to collaborate and get new ideas from others.

A Stay at Home Renewal

- Sally is a ghostwriter for corporate CEOs and high level managers. She was making money, but was not happy. Her stress level was so severe that her physical health had deteriorated. She didn't want to take extended time-off away from home because she didn't want to leave her husband. For six months she saved, developed a financial plan, and cut down her daily expenses so that she could take time-off.

Part of her renewal program was to get into better physical shape by working out regularly. She gave herself time to daydream, do nothing, and return to her childhood hopes and painting.

Writing fiction is a dream she wanted to fulfill. After two months, she signed up for a fiction writing class. Between her class and reflective time, her creativity began to flow. Her writing was highly successful. She emerged from her renewal healthier and ready to write her first fiction book. She says, "choosing the work you love is important."

Renewal Worksheet and Assessment

This assessment offers a starting point for stimulating renewal time dreams and ideas. Add in some of your own ideas under the following categories. Remember, you can combine more than one category—such as travel, studying, developing a new skill, and learning about a culture. In fact, several can be combined if you decide to volunteer. Work-study is an inexpensive way of taking time-off.

Renewal Categories

Physical—Hike the Appalachian Trail

Spiritual—Attend a spiritual retreat

Intellectual—Study environmental sciences

New Skills—Cooking or art courses in Italy

Volunteering—Helping with reforestation

Work-Study—Apprentice with a craftsman

Travel—Learn about a culture

Questions about Health and Language

Ask yourself:

- What is my current health status?

- Is my destination a realistic place considering my health?

- Can I realistically learn some language before going?

- If I choose a foreign destination, do I possess sufficient language skills or can I develop them?

Finish this sentence: "If only I had time, I would_____."

Chapter 12

Successfully Pulling the Plug

In preparing for battle I have always found that plans are useless, but planning is indispensable.
—Dwight D. Eisenhower

*I*n the last chapter, we discussed goals and strategies for planning your time-off. Now you are ready to consider tactics and timetables. The 12-Month Time-Line Chart countdown begins where we left off in the last chapter.

Minus 9 Months—Affordability

By now, you must be asking the pressing question, how will I pay for all this? In our case, we implemented a plan that wouldn't strap us financially—and your goal should be similar. The objective here is to plan creatively so that all your savings aren't tapped and you don't have to go into debt.

One of the first steps we took was to prepare a budget comparable to our current and projected living expenses. There is a chart that includes the following items (and many others). This chart will assist you in calculating your Income/Expense Budget.

- Rent
- Food
- Phone
- Electricity
- Insurance

Next, we made a list of expenses for services we didn't need while out of the country such as car expenses, insurance, vacation money, clothes, magazine subscriptions, etc. We cut all those that were unnecessary.

Instead of leaving our home vacant, we determined that by renting our home we could supplement our income. In turn, this would help to pay for our monthly living expenses while traveling. Our research indicated that in our four destinations, except for Japan, the cost of living would probably be less than our normal budget at home. If we lived on a modest budget, which included using buses and trains instead of renting a car, we would probably get by without dipping into savings or adding more debt. In addition, we decided to take on volunteer work that would cover room and board in the more expensive countries.

Our overall advice on the topic of affordability? Spend enough time to accurately determine your current expenses and your traveling needs. Then, be prepared to think creatively on how to finance your trip. Look for opportunities to supplement your income while away. Be willing to live more modestly. If you currently rent, does it make sense for you to sublet? Or, would your financial objectives best be met by ending your lease and putting your belongings into storage? If you own a condo, what are the rules for subletting? Be careful not to overlook any detail that may derail your plan.

Airfare travel costs change by the minute. Do a lot of research before settling on one price. Our travel agent was able to get us a "round-the-world" ticket at a cost of $2,900 per person. This type of fare is completely time flexible—you can change the dates of arrival and departure as long as you keep to the designated route. Because of our itinerary, we were able to use United Airlines and its Star Alliance carriers. Consider your destination sequence carefully when you are planning multiple countries. Believe it or not, it could make the difference between a $3,000 and a $40,000 ticket!

Anticipate spending some extra fare on air, bus, or rail lines. Depending on your budget, there is flexibility for traveling around a point of destination along the way. We made three significant changes along the way after weighing objectives against costs.

Who Will Handle Your Work/Business While Away?

Small Business Owner

- If you are a small business owner, you may need to put elaborate systems into place to keep the business doors open. For example, I began training a trusted associate to handle the administrative work for my consulting business a year in advance. Her main responsibility was to answer all voice mail and then delegate work to other designated consultants. Before leaving, I met with the three consultants who would do the actual work. They all signed contracts clarifying their responsibilities.

As things turned out, the communication between them was excellent and many jobs were fulfilled. I kept track of work assignments through e-mail correspondence. I was able to answer questions as they came up. All in all, I was very satisfied with the procedure. If you are a small business owner, you might want to consider using employees currently on staff who can be trained to handle assignments. Another possibility is to consider joining forces with another company during your leave. Whatever you do, make sure there are clear written agreements so there are no misunderstandings during your leave—and when you return.

Independent Consultant

- If you are an independent consultant your situation may depend on the kind of work you do. Michael is quite portable with his project work, so long as limited client and colleague interface is required. Since the laptop would accompany us, all project information would be readily available. He informed each client and indicated that follow-ups were possible, but he did not encourage new projects. Those usually require face-to-face time. He noted, "besides, what's the point of time-off if you continue in the same old mode." Still, he made it clear that he did not want to close off any bridges for future consideration. Even independent consultants can arrange for others to handle clients while they are gone.

There are obviously many other individual situations. And as discussed in the last chapter, there are creative negotiations required with managers and colleagues for how to handle work while away. Remember that nobody is indispensable.

Financial Planner Worksheet
Budget:

Expenses				
	Week	Month	Annual	Basis
Mortgage				
P&I/Rent				
Property Tax				
Utilities				
Electric				
Gas				
Water				
Tel./Cable				
Cleaning				

	Week	Month	Annual	Basis
Security Newspaper Misc.				
Maintenance & Repair				
Total Household Expense				
Food				
Restaurant/ Take-out				
Entertainment				
Personal & Household				

Automobile
    Upkeep
    Gas/Oil
    Finance Charge				

Total Auto				

Insurance
    Home
    Auto
    Life
    Dental
    Health				

Total Insurance				
Prescription Medical Glasses Unreimbursed				

	Week	Month	Annual	Basis
Health Club				
Clothing				
Discretionary				
Gifts				
Charity				
Religion				
Education				
Travel				
IRA's				
Savings				
Total Discretionary				
TOTAL EXPENSE:				

Income Sources:				
	Before Tax	Tax	After Tax	Monthly After Tax
Jobs				
Real Estate				
Loans				
Interest & Dividend				
Other				
Total:				
Investment Sources:				
Bank, CDs				
Stocks, Bonds				
Max. Available After Tax:				

Options for Financing Your Trip

- This is obviously an important area to research. Be creative in your approach. Think of combining one or more ways. Remember the goal is to have some time-off to renew and recharge yourself! Here are some ideas that may help you finance your trip and realize your renewal dreams.

1. Use some savings.

2. Cash in a life insurance policy.

3. Work as you go (For example, we met a man who was a plumber and had been doing odd jobs around the world. Everyone needs a plumber).

4. Study or apply yourself to something your company will pay for.

5. House sit.

6. Volunteer for room and board.

7. Write off some of the trip—use the trip to enhance a current or new business career. For example, I wrote articles while on the road and integrated the experience into my current business.

8. Obtain a grant.

9. Take a loan.

10. Stay with global members of an association to which you belong. (American Society for Training and Development, National Speakers Association, etc.).

11. Use investment income.

12. Join an international exchange organization such as Servas. You offer a room for a few nights to someone in exchange for stays in their home.

13. Use pension income.

14. Find a sponsor in exchange for a story or testimonial about their product—Kodak (film), Eddie Bauer (outdoor equipment).

15. Exchange houses.

16. Make a list of how you can reduce expenses while traveling such as not having a car, using hostels instead of hotels, cooking in, doing your own laundry, traveling by bike, and living with families, etc.

17. Use travel tips from experienced travelers.

18. Use your network of friends and associates and learn more about various ways to prepare for a long trip. For us, renewal preparation during this time included reading available books, searching the web, and networking with others who have taken time-off.
(See Resources)

Assessing Your Travel Personality

How much comfort do you need? Are you a princess or a rough rider? Rate yourself by answering the questions below.

The Prince/Princess

You need first class tickets, hotels, and restaurants. You rarely walk anywhere. Air conditioning is a must when it's hot. You can't do without a nice hot bath/shower and total privacy. A car is a must. You like mints on your pillow. Advice: Unless you are wealthy, extended time-off may not be for you. Take a long, luxurious vacation instead.

Average Joe/Jane

You need some hot water and heat, or air conditioning occasionally, but are willing to rough it to save money and for the travel experience.

Advice: It won't be too hard to plan a trip on a budget.

The Rough Rider

Sleep anywhere, eat anything, willing to walk, willing to work. Advice: You will have many more options be-

> cause of your flexibility. You'll need very little spending money.

Minus 6 Months—Personal Affairs

Only when you begin to hit the pause button do you realize how complex your life really is. For starters, there are monthly bills to be paid, banking, and income that needs attending to. Then, let's not forget about Uncle Sam and the IRS. Fortunately, there are many ways to tackle your personal affairs while away. As the half way point to our leaving arrived, we were faced with the arduous task of setting up systems for handling personal finances—continuation of income sources, paying bills, preparing for income taxes, and setting up communication services.

There are accounting firms and small business services that will handle your affairs for you. Or, you could negotiate with a friend who is reliable, organized, and has the time. Luckily, my sister and her husband, who happens to be an accountant, agreed to handle our affairs. We did pay them an hourly fee. Keep in mind that this is a very time-consuming activity and I wouldn't recommend asking favors. When you are away for a year, it is a relief to have a competent and close family member to oversee the many, and sometimes complicated responsibilities, which includes having access to income sources, bank accounts, and safe deposit boxes.

How will you receive mail? There are many options and a lot depends on where you are going, how long you will be in one place, and how much you can take care of on the Internet. You can have mail sent/forwarded to an American Express post office in a country you are living in. Or, you can put it on hold and have someone such as a friend, family, or associate pick it up once a month and send it to you by Federal Express, US postal office, or other mail services. You can also have it forwarded free of charge to a post office in the States by using the US postal change of address kits. Mail can be forwarded for up to one year. Mail can also be forwarded overseas but you will have to incur costs for the international postage. There are professional mailing services such as Mail Boxes, Etc. that collect mail from a post office box or their address and then forward it to you. If you will be in one location, then you can simply have the mail forwarded to that location.

Other details you will need to attend to are magazine subscriptions, annual reports, and package deliveries. Packages will cost a lot more to send to a foreign country. Also, check out the rules for receiving packages. Are there custom duties? If so, you might get around it by having them marked as "gifts." If you use a mail forwarding service, anticipate paying for a post office box as well as the mail forwarding system.

Whatever option you choose be sure to determine when you need to get the bills in order to pay them on time. Set up automatic bill payment with as many providers as possible. This will reduce administration considerably. Alternatively set up Internet payment capability either with your bank or directly with all possible providers. In our case my sister paid the bills by mail. Take the time to investigate a variety of available services in your area and the costs. There are some services that are franchised and have overseas experience.

Make a list of everyone you need to notify such as suppliers, utilities, doctors, lawyers, banks, insurance companies, stockbrokers, credit card companies, etc. In our case, Michael called to have the proper set-up for e-mail and web site connectivity for accessing accounts. Make sure you have the right software and can access anywhere in the world.

Since our trip was taken, it seems even easier to access accounts and pay bills through the Internet. Make sure providers are accessible. Paying bills and making deposits via bank arrangements can ease these transactions considerably.

Minus 4 Months—Communications Systems

When it comes to phone service, you'll need to think about what you need to keep activated at home. This could include such things as voice mail and what is required while traveling. There are many possibilities. Do you rent or buy a cell phone? Do you set up a phone account to access in other countries? Do you use a call back system?

It was necessary for us to have both special phone services at home and abroad. For practical reasons, Michael's business phone was put on a three-month Movers Voice Mail (Ameritech, $52.00). After that, the phone line was disconnected. It made sense to put my business telephone line on a permanent voice mail. My assistant checked in daily for messages ($35.00 a month, Ameritech). For our international calls, the cheapest and easiest service was the AT&T direct billed international calling card. In some countries, though, you may find that phone cards are cheaper and work well.

How will you pay your phone bills? We had our telephone bills mailed to my sister. However, this arrangement turned into a disaster when a bill was lost in the mail. We couldn't make calls for two weeks. Since our return, paying bills through a bank account with the Internet has improved.

Be sure you understand all the conditions before you sign up for a service. AT&T failed to explain their $150 maximum cap and our long distance service was turned down several times during the trip. Getting all the correct information is never easy. The communication services change so often that it is best to call and find out what is new and available.

AT&T offers English language translation services, a message service in foreign countries and many others. Determine what you need and call to find out what is most practical and cost efficient. On our return we had to pay new line costs for the phone lines that were disconnected. Check out the rules and rates before leaving.

Cell Phones

Mobile phones sold in the US are incompatible with communications networks in other countries. AT&T Wireless does offer the choice of renting or buying through WorldConnect program. There are some new companies that now offer short-term rentals. (See Resources at the end of chapter.) You can prearrange for rentals or, in some instances, look for international airports that have kiosks where you can rent phones. These services improve regularly and more offerings are available each year. You will have to research when you are ready to investigate the possibility.

The rentals aren't cheap and are definitely more expensive that using a prepaid phone card. Charges also vary when you travel from country to country. We rented a cell phone several years ago for a trip to Italy. The phone company was located in England, so each time we called them for help we were paying the charges from England. Many times the service didn't work and when we called in for assistance, we were charged the long distance rate. To our surprise, we were also charged for getting our messages. Imagine our shock when the bill came to over $1,000 for only four weeks. During that time, we only made a dozen or so calls. The other consideration is that many cell phones don't work when you are in the mountains or remote locations. I remember standing on a rooftop in a rented home in Sicily trying to call my mother.

However, if you are traveling alone, you may feel more secure with a cell phone. We had no desire to be so accessible to friends, family, and co-workers. At any rate, check the possibilities and determine your needs before deciding.

Computers and the Internet

Will you need a computer, or can you manage with Internet cafes? We determined that our need for regular communication was important and we wanted to keep good notes on our trip, so we invested in a laptop (Sony VAIO, thin and weighing 3 lb. with a cable and lock) a perfect size for a backpack.

You may need additional equipment for many countries where you travel. We purchased telephone modem connections and electric adapters for each country as needed. These devices are available in travel stores as well as online through travel resources such as Travel Smith (www.travelsmith.com). Walkabout Travel Gear answered many of our questions as well (www.walkabouttravelgear.com/wwelect.htm), and have everything you may need. For security in hotels, we used a cable which fit in the laptop and then hooked around a pipe or bedpost. The Internet access and e-mail was an invaluable link to home and work, as Cybernet cafes aren't always available in small towns.

If you don't bring a computer or the hotel connection doesn't connect properly, you can try to locate a Cybernet cafe or other resources. Some airports now offer Internet access, and many large hotels have a business center. Hotel charges are usually higher than cafes. Check out www.netcafeguide.com, www.cybercafes.com, and www.cybercaptive.com for listings of locations and Hotmail. As we found out, many libraries and universities have connections as well. In several instances the university was extremely helpful to us as foreign travelers needing to make contact with home. In Japan, it was so hard to read signs and that we mistakenly ended up in a business establishment selling computers and software. The manager was so hospitable that he let us use his personal computer. The best advice is to be resourceful and ask people for help. Eventually, something will turn up.

After researching Internet providers who have service overseas, we settled on AOL. As phone services change, so do Internet service providers, and you will want to settle on the one that is cost efficient and yet available in countries where you will be traveling. Domestic and local providers can't support internationally. Even AOL had limitations in that we had to pay surcharges for many locations and experienced slow transmission speeds.

Here is a bit of advice on surcharges. When we connected using our AOL provider (from our apartments in Spain and Switzerland), we tried to set time limits on surfing because of the considerable surcharges. When using Internet cafes, you are usually charged only by time use and it is less expensive.

Palm Pilots and Other Gadgets

Palm pilots were still not widely used when we prepared for our trip. We typed in addresses, phone numbers, and other vital information and stored them in a database on our computers. I used a most low-tech device, a gift of a Japanese miniature address book (2"x 4") where I wrote down important phone, address, visa, airline information, etc. I still have it and prefer it to palm pilots. We also carried a back-up paper copy of our visa numbers, and emergency information in our security pouches that went around our waists and then was tucked into our pants. A tip for females—I never carried a purse, preferring to use the inside pockets on my jacket and our backpacks instead.

Wireless Internet devices are available now and can be useful. However, one of our goals was to get away from technology except our PC. Technology can become something else to worry about and protect. In the end, you will have to determine what works best for you.

Trip Preparation

Preparing for a long trip has some similarities to going on a vacation, such as health coverage, insurance, international driving permits, passports, traveler's checks, vocabulary books, etc. Who will care for the car, yard or snow removal while your are gone?

Our process was the same. We checked passports and clarified visa information. We purchased $1,000 worth of traveler's checks (two-signers), but ATM for cash was most convenient everywhere but Japan. I also began a Spanish language class while Michael dusted off his Spanish vocabulary books.

Putting our health needs in order was next on the list—setting up doctor and dentist checkups, and clarifying health coverage abroad. Our private insurance covered our doctor visits so we didn't need additional coverage. Check with your health care provider to see if you are covered. I did apply for an international list of recommended doctors and hospitals from the International Association for Medical Assistance to Travelers. If you don't have health coverage away from home, you may consider some options such as Access America, International SOS Assistance, and Medex. (See Resources)

Don't forget prescriptions. I filled a whole year's worth of one medication. In many countries, it is easy to get medications at a pharmacy without a prescription. Pharmacies are also good places to get a recommendation for a doctor. This was the case when I contracted a skin fungus in Japan, which was easily remedied.

If you are traveling to Nepal or other areas that are remote, you may want to research Emergency Medical Evacuation Insurance. If you ever need recovery from those remote regions, it could cost you tens of thousands of dollars without the insurance. SOS and Medex are two providers that sell the insurance.

To avoid unnecessary surprises, keep a list of US consulates or embassies in the country you are visiting. Each time we settled in a new city, I also got into a routine of checking out the phone numbers of local hospitals and other emergency numbers. We never had to use them, but it gave me a sense of security. Tourist bureaus are good places to get all those numbers.

What will you do with your car while you are away? Car storage rates were anywhere from $50 to $100 per month depending on the service (heated garage, etc.). Fortunately for us, friends came to our aid and offered to take one car and the other was stored in our garage and was driven for us every month. These situations saved us money on storage cost, as well as saving our car tires and battery.

We also applied for international driving permits. International driving permits are useful if there is an accident or a troublesome border crossing. In fact, they are mandatory in some countries. We recommend you apply for one. It's an easy process through the American Automobile Association. The cost is only $10.

What about your pet? We do not have any so it wasn't an issue. You can ask someone to care for it for while you are away or you can check into taking your pet with you. On a former trip, my parents kept my dog for a year. Check with the consulate or embassy of the country you are visiting for special rules. The airlines allow pets less than seventeen pounds to travel as carry-on luggage. Be sure to get clarification beforehand.

Minus 3 Months—House/Apartment Rental Process

If you decide to rent out your home or apartment, you can do it yourself or hire a realtor. It depends on how much time you have to take care of the details. Or, you might combine both options. Including a realtor in your plan—one who can market and is familiar with contracts—is an advantage, but at the cost of a month's rent. No matter what you decide, be sure to take the time to check out your future tenants. It was one of our biggest mistakes.

We put an ad in the local paper, signs up at the nearby university, and worked with a real estate agent. We synchronized the beginning of our trip with the school year, thus making it easier to find a one-year tenant for our house. There was a miscommunication and the agent didn't start looking for us until a month before the departure date. The pressure was now greater to find a tenant and, as a result, we ended up just taking someone in lieu of waiting for the right person. Our mistake was paid for heavily at the end of the year when the tenant vacated early without notification and left a hefty mess behind. If we had to do it again, we would still rent. However, we would start early enough to find the right tenant.

Who will watch over your home and yard even if you rent? If you own a home or other property, it is necessary to have an emergency contact. We were fortunate to have Michael's son, Mark, to oversee the property. He is also a general contractor and familiar with likely problems. Having reliable individuals to check on things occasionally will also provide peace of mind.

Packing Preparation Guidelines

Deciding what to pack is a very important process. After all, you are going away for an extended time, and you want to make sure you have packed things that you can't get in other countries. It's nice to have a few special things that make you feel comfortable, like your favorite walking shoes, reading materials, or outfit. It is always a challenge if you are traveling with a partner. There will be differences and compromises. Michael's goal was to keep the weight under 50 lbs. We also agreed that each of us would be responsible for our own luggage. Our golden rule was, "If you can carry it, you can take it!"

If you are like us, start early enough so you can think through each and every item and reevaluate its value and necessity. We probably repacked mentally about ten times and then made trials. We rearranged and took out items right up to the day of departure. Give yourself permission to go through this process until you are comfortable

To carry our belongings, we settled on a three-foot canvas bag (made by Eagle Creek) on solid rollers and with a retractable handle for each of us plus a small backpack each. We spent many hours in the travel luggage department trying these out. You can see your options on the Internet, but we recommend you take the time to look at them in person. Travel Smith and Eddie Bauer are good options to check out. One of the backpacks was larger and could supplement as an overnighter or for short side trips. We ended up using the larger backpack (Eagle Creek) often for trips up to two weeks duration.

Packing Tips for a Year

Here are suggestions from our experience. Keep in mind that after a while you won't notice your clothes. You will be too busy exploring. Traveling with less will make your trip easier and more enjoyable. If possible plan your itinerary, so you travel in the same season. It is a lot easier to pack for summer than it is for winter and summer. If not possible, seasonal shipments can be arranged. (As we did.)

Purchase one piece of luggage with wheels.

Take two of everything (except for more underwear and socks).

Purchase two pair of silk or thermal underwear for winter.

Leave heavy shampoo/conditioner, books, paper—buy at destination.

Think layers and dark colors (you don't want to stand out).

Purchase the best socks and walking shoes.

Pack everything and then unload half.

Practice going up and down the stairs with luggage. Remember you have to carry it! There are many train stations that don't have elevators or escalators, especially in Japan. Also, many lodgings will only have stairs.

Take good rain gear (mine had an inner lining which doubles as a light jacket).

For women, bring a few scarves to brighten daily wear. Leave jewelry at home. Use a separate backpack for carry-on and short trips. We stored our big suitcases in lockers at train and bus stations or, when possible, in lodgings. In Spain we had an apartment which made short trips very convenient and a provided a safe place to keep our belongings.

Take a water bottle with a strap.

Pack clothes and organize generally in large clear plastic zip lock bags.

Take a diskette with important contacts for backup plus a paper copy of important information.

Photo copy all travel documents, passports, birth certificates, marriage license, prescriptions, insurance, and medical history.

Pack a good first aid kit (antibiotics, ibuprophen, antifungal crème, bed bug spray, sunscreen, etc.).

Except for third world countries, you can buy most necessities at your destination.

Take hats for sun and/or warmth.

Pack a camera. If you plan to send photos via Internet, think about a digital. Otherwise, be practical and make it small and light. You can always buy Kodak disposable camera if you don't want to be encumbered.

Film—we bought several rolls ahead of time because in some countries, film is very expensive. Think ahead on how you will use your photos. Are you planning slide shows? This will make a difference when you return home. Also, due to weight and risk of loss consider shipping photos home. We separated photos and negatives and sent them in different boxes. We didn't want to lose our trip memories.

> Books—they can be your best companion on a trip. Pack those that will bring you comfort. Even though heavy, we made them a priority.
> In summation, travel light and simple but meet essential needs. It will enhance your travel experience.

Minus 2 Months—Packing the Household

Leaving your house or apartment for a year is a great opportunity for you to pare down. Allow sufficient time to pack and sort out your possessions.

Packing the household items and business files took us a month. It was a good chance to discard many things we didn't need anymore. Cleaning out files and unused clothing was also mentally cleansing and formed the beginning steps toward leading a more simple lifestyle. We saved storage costs by leaving many items in our basement (our renter consented to this).

Think Ahead

It's hard to think ahead to the future while you are packing to leave but it is important to ensure the continuation of your work life when you return. To prepare for leaving my business, I sent out a business Press Release and set up a special "Time-Off" section on my business web site.

Think ahead as much as possible to all your needs for the coming year, including such quarterly or annual events as income taxes. Don't forget to enter all-important information in your computer as well as some paper backups. During this period of constructive chaos, we also backed up computer files, prepared 1099's ahead of time for subcontractors.

Miscellaneous Preparation Details

You mean there's more? Yes, and these are essential details that need attending to. This includes delegating responsibility for handling of other real estate properties or assets you have. In advance, send a change of address. We did it a month early to make sure the mail would be properly forwarded to my sister. Be sure to photocopy passports, tickets, birth certificates, and a marriage license. Also, cancel unnecessary car insurance, stop newspaper and magazine subscriptions, and discontinue your cable service, Lastly, get traveler's checks, buy film, and fill any necessary prescriptions. Whew! You may suddenly realize what a complicated life you live. We were looking forward to giving up some of the responsibilities and living simpler lives.

You can count on forgetting to do something before you leave. Relax and realize you can probably take care of it by phone, fax, e-mail, or with the help of a friend. One of the big lessons in preparing for the trip is finding we aren't perfect, but we do have skills to deal with issues as they arise. Still, it is impossible to plan for absolutely everything, and if you could it might take away some of the serendipity. In fact, part of an adventure for us is not to know everything up front. Problem solving and being flexible was key to our trip as you discovered in prior chapters Some of you may need more structure to feel comfortable. You may want to have more details planned in advance than we did.

Minus 1 Month—Saying Good Bye

You will suddenly realize it is time to say adios. Be sure to give yourself enough time to do it properly. Good byes are part of the transition to the next experience. We took lots of time to say good bye to clients, friends, and family. My daughter and family visited us for a week. Then, we gave a party and asked our friends to take a memory item from our home. The idea is to let trusted friends/family choose something from our home as a way of keeping us in their daily thoughts. It could be a special sugar bowl, picture, or plant.

This was also a useful way of dealing with storage of precious household and personal items. Our good friends took many paintings, rugs, ceramics, and silver. It was a good way for our friends to have a part of us while we were away.

Ready, set, go. Before you know it is time to leave. How will you make the final transition? We moved out three days early and stayed with a friend. This gave us time to relax and to focus on the trip. It was a time of high emotion. However, we never questioned whether or not we were doing the right thing. We knew we had made a good and important decision about our lives. We had hit the pause button and now we were about to enter the new phase of exploration, searching our passions, and renewing our spirit.

Here's a thumbnail summary of the whole Time Line Chart and process of preparation.

Communications

What do you need? Here's a handy checklist.

Phones—
- Cell phone—rental vs. purchase
- Notify everyone
- Phone—connection at home?
- Hold
- Phone cards
- Voice mail
- Other

Snail Mail—
- Forward or hold

Electronic Connectivity—
- Determine what is needed
- Computer, peripherals, etc.
- Modem adapters
- Electric plugs
- Surge protector
- Security lock

Internet Options—
- Own computer and service provider
- Cybercafe
- Hotels
- Libraries
- Universities

Time Line Chart Summary

Minus 12 Months
Decision making—can we do this?

Minus 11 Months
Consider options for time-off—what, where, how, when.

Minus 10 Months
Make your choices for where.

Minus 9 Months
Determine how you will finance the time-off.
If you are a business owner, how will you keep the business going? Plan to notify, negotiate with job options.

> **Minus 8-6 Months**
> Establish budgets.
>
> **Minus 6–3 Months**
> Begin process for handling personal affairs (mail, communications at home and away, paying bills, house/apt. rental, car/furniture storage, language study, visas, passports, travel gear, pets).
> Health check ups.
> Practice packing.
>
> **Minus 2 Months**
> Pack household items.
> Details of personal affairs (change of address, photocopying passports, birth certificates, canceling unnecessary insurance, stopping newspapers, magazine subscriptions, cable).
>
> **Minus 1 Month**
> Say good byes.
> Mental preparation.

Lessons Learned

- Take time to interview the right renters for your home/apartment.

- Start language study earlier and study hard.

- Pack fewer clothes.

- Always keep sight of the goals.

- Recognize that problems will come along the way but that none are insurmountable.

- Trust in your plan.

- You are not going to the moon.

Dare to Dream

It is possible at any age to fulfill dreams. Never give them up because it is our dreams that sustain us. Don't wait too long to act on your dreams. Time has a way of getting away from us and one day it will be too late.

Dream, act, live, recharge, and rekindle the passion in your life!

Chapter 13

Renewal Tips, Workshops, and Resources

If You Can't Go Away: Daily Tips for Renewal

Take time out for some reflection, even if it is only ten minutes a day. Once you are home avoid checking in immediately with e-mail and voice mail. Cut down on TV and the Internet and take a walk instead. When at work, find a time to rest your eyes for a few minutes during the day. Be present moment by moment instead of thinking about the past or the future. Teach your family ways to be reflective and don't over program yourself or family. Keep it simple

Experiment with taking a little adventure, such as something that will promote risk taking. If you are used to taking tours, go on your own for a half a day and stretch those problem solving skills. If you are traveling in a foreign country, learn a few words and don't be embarrassed to try them out.

Get our of the comfort zone for a short time. Try staying in a rustic environment without all the creature comforts of home. Give yourself a little challenge.

Try something you have always wanted to do but were afraid to try, like salsa dancing, snorkeling, and canoeing. You may not be perfect at whatever you undertake but the efforts count for your renewal. You will feel better about your risk-taking skills. Make some new connections by hosting a foreign visitor for a short time. Use the resources of Servas or the Friendship Force.

Volunteer at a local organization, such as homeless shelters, soup kitchens, and Habitat for Humanity. One of our friends recently read about a Pakistani family needing help and they hosted them for Thanksgiving. The local newspapers found out and did a story. The ripple effect was tremendous. Through the media exposure, the couple was able to get work, furniture, and new connections in their life. The family that extended themselves was revitalized because they extended themselves to help others.

Focus on things you already possess. Be grateful everyday for what you have. Just expressing your gratitude out loud when you rise in the morning or at meal time can reduce the stress in your life and provide a continuous stream of renewal. Try living more simply. Assess what you really need in your life and be aware of your impulses to accumulate more. Does it really add value to your life to buy more?

Oprah and Renewal

My ideas are supported by Oprah in her pursuit of renewal. The July, 2001 Issue of "O" featured an article on Oprah's 'mini-sabbatical." The article is devoted to her weekend of silent meditation and how it can help to renew readers. She points out the importance of "time out" in small ways. "it is critical that we cut everything off from time to time—that we unplug the phone, let the e-mail pile up, and send the kids off to a friend's house. Our real power comes from knowing who we are and what we're here to do. And that begins with looking inside ourselves in silence. Solitude is part of the path to spiritual awareness."

You may be able to see the value of using these reflective techniques even if you can't go away for a longer period of time. By incorporating practices of "time-off" in small ways and learning to explore the inner self through silence and meditation practices, you may find it easier to cope with the day to day stresses of ongoing change. Not only are these techniques good for individuals but are also excellent for parents and their families. (*Inward Bound*, O, The Oprah Magazine, Oprah Winfrey, July, 2001)

Renewal Workshop Offerings

After being back for several months, I realized the value of what we learned and began to share it in presentations and workshops for both businesses and individuals. The process we went through was reflective and involved self-awareness and self-discovery. These are important skills for renewal.

The first thing I did was to hold a "Leadership Renewal Retreat" six months after returning by bringing work-life professionals together for a day of renewal—a day to discuss their leadership role as well as learning techniques to control the stress in their lives. Stress has an affect on their ability to be creative and to be work-life champions.

The response for the first public workshop was very good and I have expanded them as world events changed. As described, the many skills we learned from our year away help to build resilience. This is particularly important now, in the aftermath of a national crisis.

Renewal, Leadership and Passion Workshops

Here are some descriptions of the presentations and workshops to promote different benefits and aspects of renewal.

Taking the Path Less Traveled

- A presentation that is entertaining and filled with thought provoking stories with personal triumphs as Bonnie recreates her year-long inner and outer journey and a little flamenco.

Sabbatical Realities and Dreams

- A nuts and bolts presentation providing vital information on taking time off.

Workshops for Professional and Personal Renewal

- Leadership Renewal for Work-Life Professionals/ Human Resource Managers

- This is an opportunity for work-life professionals to come together with a focus on acknowledging our work-life successes along with replenishing their leadership role with passion. This workshop provides opportunities for enhancing leadership and managing with resilience.

Managers/Supervisors Who Manage the Changing Workforce

- This workshop is designed to assist you in having well-developed emotional intelligence with benefits of:

- Understanding the emotional makeup of other people.

- Renewing your passion to work

- Finding common ground and building rapport

- Negotiating flexibility

Beyond Balance

- This workshop is for individuals in stressful work-life situations.

- You will find deeper ways to meet the work-life challenges and set the tone for what you want to happen.

- The passion for your life can be rekindled and you will leave with tools to transform your world from the ordinary into the extraordinary.

For more information contact:

Bonnie Michaels
912 Crain Street
Evanston, IL 60202
847/864-0916
www.mwfam.com, www.bonniemichaels.com

Renewal Resources

Travel Companies

- Air Brokers International (800) 883-3273
  www.airbrokers.com

- Travel Companion
  www. Travelcompanions.com
  www.whytravelalone.com

- Air Treks
  (800) 350-0636, www.airtreks.com

- Other on-line consolidators—
  www.Onetravel.com, hotwire.com
  Elder Treks (800) 741-7956, www.eldertreks.com

- Specialty Travel Index
  Tour operators who feature unusual opportunities.
  (415-459-4900), www.luptrael.com

- Ocean Voyages, Inc.
  Places you aboard a yacht or charter sailboats.
  (415) 3324681

- League of American Cyclists
  Allows members' bicycles to fly free.
  (800) 288-2453, www.bikeleague.org

- Other Biking –www. actionsites.com

Cell Phone Information

- AT&T-WorldConnect program (rent or buy)

- Roberts Rent-a-Phone, New York (888) 802-9618, www.roberts-rent-aphone.com

- Cellhire (888) 246-6546, www.cellhire.com

- WorldCell (888) 967-323, www.worldcell.com

- InTouch Global (800) 872-7626, www.worldcell.com

- Roadpost (888) 290-1616, www.roadpost.com

- Planetfone (888) 988-4777, www.planetfone.com

- Nextel (800) 639-8359, www.nextel.com

Travel Gear

- TravelSmith- travel supplies
  www.travelsmith.com

- Walkabout Gear-travel supplies
  (800) 274-4277
  www.walkabouttravelgear.com/wwelect.htm

- Eagle Creek Travel supplies
  www.eaglecreek.com

- TravelProducts.Com- Jet lag remedy, improved sleep mask, travel games, pop-up maps, travel software, adapters, modems, and mini hair-dryer.
  www.travelproducts.com

- Travel Supplies
  www.travelsupplies.com

- Korjo Travel Products- Australian-based company offering a range of travel accessories. Site provides travel tips and checklists.
  www.korjo.com

- Executive Travelware, Inc.- Travel accessories, luggage, globes, clocks and gifts plus tips and links.
  www.travelwares.com

- Cirrus Health Care Products- Provides travel, safety and personal healthcare products to relieve ear pain from in flight pressure, motion sickness and dental care products.
  www.cirrushealthcare.com

- eTravelerGear -Travel products and accessories for frequent and business travelers.
  www.etravelergear.com

- Radio Shack- Adapters, converters, transformers
  www.radioshack

- Magellans- Catalog Travel products
  (800) 962-4943, www.magellans.com

- Traveling with Children- Travel tips and information as well as a range of products for traveling with babies and young children.
  www.travellingwithchildren.co.uk

- Travelelectronics.com- International plug adapters, phone jacks, transformers, regulators and health products for the traveler.
  www.travelelectronics.com

- Country Trails- A range of travel products; clothing and equipment for camping, walking, mountaineering, and skiing.
  www.countrytrails.co.uk

- Dental Kit for Travelers- A compact dental kit to handle dental emergencies while traveling.
  www.dentalkitfortravelers.com

- The Mouse- A portable, freestanding door lock for personal security while traveling.
  www.themouse.org.uk

- TravelStore24 - Hairdryers, weather monitoring, travel games, suitcases and toothbrushes.
  www.travelstore24.co.uk

- On The Go Travel Accessories- Accessories for personal and business travel including luggage, organizer bags, business cases and auto accessories.
  www.onthegoaccessories.com

- Avid- Headsets, headphones, passenger amenity kits and other airline travel products.
  www.avid-travel.com

- Family Vacation Store- Toys, coolers, outdoor needs, chairs and hammocks, knives and other accessories for family travel.
  www.familyvacationstore.com

- The Nielsen Way- A personal organizer that fits under a jacket and accommodates office and travel items.
  www.thenielsenway.com

- Vacation Gadgetman- Gadgets for the beach, pool, camping, winter along with stuff for the kids and electronic gadgets.
  www.vacationgadgetman.com

Homestay Programs

- American-International Homestays
  Places with English-speaking hosts
  (800) 876-2048, www.spectravel.com/homes

- AmeriSpan
  Language and homestays (Latin American Countries)
  (800) 879-6640
  www.amerispan.com;infor@amerispan.com

- Elderhostels
 For individuals 55+, combines homestays with non-credit academic courses and field trips.
 (617) 426-7788, www.elderhostel.org

- LEX Amerian
 Homestays for adults and families including students in Japan and Korea. You travel there as a group and then meet your host family. You can host visitors to the US.
 (617) 489-5800, www.lexlrf.com

- Seniors Abroad
 Homestays for 50+ in Japan, New Zealand/Australia
 (619) 485-1696, www.myprimetime.com

- Servas
 National Directories. You borrow a country list for a $25 deposit and make your own arrangements. Two days free lodging. Goal is to promote world peace.
 (212) 267-0252. www.servas.org

- The Friendship Force
 A program dedicated to world peace through a unique homestay program.
 (404) 522-9490
 www.friendship-force.org, ffi@friendship-force.org

- Transitions Abroad
 Bimonthly magazine for homestays, study programs, living and working abroad.
 www.transabroad.com

- World Learning
  Arranges one to four-week homestays in 22 countries.
  (800) 662-2967
  www.worldlearning.org

House Exchange and Rentals

- At Home Abroad
  Western Europe, Caribbean and Mexico rentals. One year registration fee.
  (212) 421-9165

- British Travel Associates
  Home rentals in Britain.
  (800) 327-6097

- Home Exchange Network
  On-line home listings.
  (407) 862-7211
  www.oas.com, www.homelink.org

- International Home Exchange Network
  Listing and posting homes.
  (805) 898-9660
  www.homexchange.com, e-mail: linda@ihen.com,

- Intervac U.S (Intervac International))
  Catalogs of home listings and some rentals. Interested people contact homeowners directly.
  (800) 756-4663, (415) 435-3497
  E-mail: IntervacUS@aol.com

- The French Experience
  Simple home rental in villages.
  (212) 986-6097, www.edexcel.org

- The Invented City
  Interntional exchange. Fee for membership.
  (800) 788-2489, www.invented-city.com
  Invented@backdoor.com

- Vacation Exchange Club
  Directories. Members call directly.
  (800) 638-384, info@vacation-inc.com

- Worldwide Exchange Club
  Directories. Members make direct contact.
  (301) 680-8950

- World-Wide Home Rental Guide
  Catalogs available for a year's subscription fee.
  (800) 299-9886, www.ihxc.com

Housesitting

- Caretaker's Gazette
  (509) 332-0806, www.angelfire.com/wa/caretaker

Work Programs

- Au Pair Homestay—US and Abroad
  Places individuals for child care work.
  (202) 408-5380
  www.undergroundtravel.com/working/legal/au-pair.htm

- The Peace Corps
  Two-year commitment for paid work in a country.
  (800) 424-8580 Ext 293, www.peacecorps.gov

- WorldTeach
  Places volunteers as teachers in developing countries. No formal teaching is required. Receive a modest fee for academic year but pay for airfare, health insurance and lodging.
  (617) 495-5527, www.igc.org/worldteach
  E-mail: Info@worldteach.org

Volunteer Programs

- Volunteers for Peace
  Inexpensive way to live and work, International Directory list programs in sixty-five countries.
  E-mail: vfp@vfp.org, www.vfp.org

- Willing Workers on Organic Farms
  Australian live and work program. Directory lists names and contact information. You make the contact.
  E-mail wwoof@net-tech.com.au, www.wwoof.org

- Earthwatch Institute
  Working with field scientists.
  (800) 776-0188, www.earthwatch.org

- Global Volunteers
  Working and living with local people on human and economic development projects.
  (800) 487-1074, www.globalvolunteers.org

- Americorps
  A government service program for 18-24 year old.
  (202) 565-2799, www.americorps

- Discussion groups for every destination and kind.
  travel www.Throntree.longlyplanet.com

On line bulletin boards

- www.about.com

- www.msn.com and www.delphi.com

- concierge.com, travelchannel.com

- Networks for Returned Volunteers (National Peace Corps Assoc.)
  (202) 293-7728, www.rcv.org,
  www.returnedvolunteers.org

Schools

- Association of Professional Schools of International Affairs. Graduate schools.
  (202) 326-7828, www.apsia.org

- Center for Global Education at Augsburg College
  (800) 299-8889, www. Augsburg.edu/global
  E-mail Globaled@augsburg.edu

- International Education and Career Resources
  www.job, www.Huntersbible.com,
  www.jobsabroad.com, www.teachabroad.com,
  www.overseas jobs.com

- Travelearn
  Learning vacations.
  (800) 235-9114, www.travelearn.com

- Language Schools
  www.languageschoolguide.com,
  www.travelsource.com/travel-schools.htm

- Teaching English in Japan
  www.Eltnews.com, wwwmofa.go.jp/j-info/visit/jet

Passports, Visa Information, Work Permits

- (800) 688-9889, www.travel.state.gov/passport_services.html

- Association for International Practical Training.
  Arranges work permits in 9 countries.
  (410) 997-2200
  www.aipt.org, e-mail aipt@aipt.org

Medical Information

- Access America
  Short term insurance coverage.
  (800) 284-8300, www.accessamer.com

- BUPA International, Russell Mews, Brighton, Great Britain BN7 2NR, United Kingdom
  Specializes in health insurance for those who live and work abroad.
  Phone: (UK) 44 1273208 181

- Blue Cross and Blue Shield of Western Europe, 59 rue de Chateaudun, 75009, Paris, France
  American Style health insurance plans.
  Phone (France) 33 1 42 81 98 76

- International SOS Assistance
  Emergency evaluation services up to 14 days.
  (800) 523-8662, www.sos.com

- Medex
  Short and long term medical assistance. Medical kits.
  (800) 537-2029, www.medexmedical.com
  E-mail: medexasst@aol.com

- Medhelp Worldwide
  Health and travel insurance to travelers who are away from their home country for at least six months.
  MW. Wallach and Company, Inc., 107 West Federal Street, P.O. Box 480, Middleburg, VA 22117, www.medhelp.org

- National Insurance Consumer Helpline,
  Sponsored through the Health Insurance Association of America.
  (800) 942-4242

- The International Association for Medical Assistance to Travelers. Directory of English speaking doctors around the world. Free membership.
  (716) 754-4883, www.sentex.net

- The International Traveler's Hotline
  Centers for Disease Control and Preventions. Information on vaccinations, precautions, etc.
  (404) 332-4559
  healthdept.co.pierce.wa.us/cdc/travellmmuh.htm

- www.healthfinder.gov/org, (888) 232-3299

- The Traveler's Emergency Network
  Offers evacuation prescription delivery anywhere. Annual membership fee.
  (800) 275-4836, www.msu.edu/~travel/hit.htm

- Travel Assistance International
  Medical assitance and limited emergency evacuation.
  (800) 821-2828, www.intmed.mcw.edu/travel.htm

- Traveled International Traveler's Assistance Association. Twenty-four hour access to Medex hotline emergency evacuation and dental coverage. Up to seventy days.
  (800) 732-5309

Lifestyle Books

Dominguez, Joe and Vicki Robin, *Your Money or Your Life*, Penguin Books, New York, 1993

Dlugozima, Hope and James Scott, and David Sharp, Henry Holt, *Six Months Off*, Henry Holt and Company, NY, 1996

Hardin, Paula Payne, *What Are You Doing With the Rest of Your Life? Choices in Midlife*, New World Library, CA, 1992

Jarvis, Cheryl, *The Marriage Sabbatical: The Journey That Brings You Home*, Perseus, 2000

Levering, Robert and Milton Moskowitz, *The One Hundred Best Companies to Work For in America*, NAL-Dutton, NY, 1994

Levey, Joel and Michelle, *Living in Balance*, Conari Press, Berkeley, CA, 1998

Mayle, Peter, *A Year in Provence*, Vintage Books, NY, 1990

Moore Thomas, *Soul Mates Honoring the Mysteries of Love and Relationship*, HarperCollins, NY, 1994

Rogak, Lisa, *Time-off From Work—Using Sabbaticals to Enhance Your Life While Keeping Your Career on Track*, John Wiley & Sons, Inc., 1994

Sharma, Robin S., *The Monk Who Sold His Ferrari—A Fable About Fulfilling Your Dreams and Reaching Your Destiny*, Harper, San Francisco, 1997

St. James, Elaine, *Simplify Your Life—110 Ways to Slow Down and Enjoy Things That Really Matter*, Hyperion, 1994

Zahorski, Kenneth J, *The Sabbatical Mentor*, 1994

Articles

Axel, Helen, *Redefining Corporate Sabbaticals for the 1990's*. New York, The Conference Board, 1992

Bachler, LeJeune, Michelle, *Sabbatical policies lacking*, Boulder County Business Report, 1996

Goodison, Donna L., Linchris *Hotel reorganizes, managers earn a 'Sabbatical,'* Boston Business Journal, August 21, 2000. http://boston.bcentral.com/boston/stories/2000/08/21/story5.html

Bachler, Christopher J., *Workers Take Leave of Job Stress*, Personnel Journal January 1995, pp.40-46

Fitzgerald, Jacqueline, *Returning Refreshed*, Chicago Tribune, WomanNews-Working, November 15, 2000

Michaels, Bonnie, *Time-off From Work and Family – Planning Your Sabbatical*, Transitions Abroad, July/August 2000

Sauer, Kurt, *The Pause That Refreshes*, (www5law.com/tx/special/salbill/03299b.htm)
Texas Lawyer, March 29, 1999

Schwartz, Shelly K. *The Corporate Sabbatical, High-tech firms embrace extended leave benefit once reserved for scholars*, CNN, November 15, 1999

Sheley Elizabeth, *Why Give Employee Sabbaticals? To Reward, Relax and Recharge, HR* Magazine, March 1996. (www.shrm.org/hrmagazine/articles/396sabb.htm)

Toomey, Edmund L. and Joan M. Connor, *Employee Sabbaticals: Who Benefits and Why,* Personnel, April 1998, pp. 81-84

Travel Books

Brown, Karen, *Country Inn Guides* series San Mateo, CA: Travel Press

Cohen, David Eliot, *One Year Off Leaving It All Behind for a Round–the–World Journey with Our Children*, Travelers' Tales Books, 2001

Church, Mike and Terri, *Traveler's Guide to European Camping*, Rolling Homes Press, Kirkland, WA, 1996

Eurail 97 Guide to Train Travel in the New Europe, Houghton Mifflin, Boston, 1997

Hampshire, David, *Living and Working in France; Living and Working in Spain; Living and Working in Britain; Living and Working in Switzerland*, Haddam, CT: Survival Books

Hasbrouck, Edward, *The Practical Nomad: How to Travel Around the World*, Avalon Travel, 2nd ed., 2001

How to Travel Without Spending a Lot of Money, John Muir Publications (800) 888-7504

Hubbs, Clayton A (General Editor) *Alternative Travel Directory, The Complete Guide To Work, Study & Travel Overseas*, Transitions Abroad Publishing, Amhert, MA, 1998

International Living Newsletter on life in various countries. E-mail 103114,2472@compuserve.com (410) 223-2619

Kohls, Robert L *Survival Kit for Overseas Living*, Intercultural Press, Yarmouth, ME, 1996

Lonely Planet Publications; 155 Filbert Street, Oakland, CA 94607

McMillon, Bill and Asner, Edward, *Volunteer Vacations, Short-Term Adventures That Will Benefit You and Others*

Stevens, Rick, *Europe Through the Back Door, Asia Through the Back Door* (Rick Stevens and Bob Effertz)

Miscellaneous Books

Peterson's Learning Adventures Around the World, edited by Peter S. Greenberg, Princeton, NJ, updated yearly

Shapiro Michael *Net Travel: How Travelers Use the Internet*, O'Reilly & Associates, Cambridge, MA, 1997

Storti, Crag, *The Art of Coming Home* (Pamphlet) www.cultureprogram.com

Names of Corporations with Sabbatical—Time-off Policies

- 3Com
- Apple Computers
- Arrow Electronics
- Du Pont Company
- Genetech, Inc.

- IBM Corportion
- Intel
- L.L. Bean
- McDonald's
- Nike
- Ralston Purina
- VLSI Technology, Inc.
- Xerox

In addition, see *Working Mothers Magazine* Annual Report on "100 Best Companies"

Flamenco Dance Resources

- www.flamencoworld.com

Archeology Resources

- Biblical Archeology, www.bib.arch.org
  www.thc.state.tx.us/TAAM/avocational.htm

Business Organizations

- Alliance for Work-Life Professionals
  www.awlp.org

- Conference Board-research, www.conferenceboard.org

- Employee Services Management Association,
  www.esm.org

- Human Resources Management Association,
  www.shrm.org

Managing Work & Family, Inc.

Since its formation in 1987 by co-founder Bonnie Michaels, the firm has a well-documented history of assisting hundreds of organizations with problem-solving strategies and creative solutions for developing comprehensive and well-integrated work-life programs. Managing Work & Family has accomplished this through a variety of cost-saving mediums such as on-site consultations, needs assessments, working with task forces, telephone conversations, publications, videos, speeches, and radio/T.V. appearances.

Bonnie Michaels is also well-known for reaching and motivating thousands of individuals with work-life balance techniques through workshops, retreats, one-on-one consultations, publications, videos, books, as well as media appearances.

Consulting Services
Renewal Workshops
Public Speaking
Flexible Manager Strategies
Employee Work-Life and Training
Work-Life Balance Retreats
Time-Off/Sabbatical Consulting and Workshops

If you would like to learn more about Bonnie Michaels' work and how it can help you, your organization or community, contact her at:

Bonnie Michaels
Managing Work & Family, Inc.
912 Crain Street, Unit B
Evanston, IL 60202
Phone: (847) 864-0916
E-mail: mwfam@aol.com
www.mwfam.com